CISTERCIAN FATHERS SERIES: NUMBER TWENTY-SIX

GILBERT OF HOYLAND

Volume Three

ON THE
SONG OF SONGS

THE WORKS OF
GILBERT *of* HOYLAND

Translated and introduced by

LAWRENCE C. BRACELAND SJ

CISTERCIAN FATHERS SERIES : NUMBER TWENTY-SIX

Sermons on the Song of Songs, III

CISTERCIAN PUBLICATIONS, INC.

KALAMAZOO, MICHIGAN 49008

1979

CISTERCIAN FATHERS SERIES

This book has been published with the help of a grant from the Canadian Federation for the Humanities, using funds provided by the Social Sciences and Humanities Research Council of Canada.

The translation here presented is based on the edition of Jean Mabillon, Milan, Gnocchi, reprint of 1852.

Original Latin title:

Sermones in Canticum Salomonis ab eo loco ubi B. Bernardus morte praeventus desiit.

The Gnocchi reprint of 1852 has been checked against the Migne reprint of 1854, *Patres Latini* 184. Discrepancies between the two reprints were checked against microfilm copies of twelfth century manuscripts: Paris, Bibliothèque National, 9605 and 8546; Bruges, Stadsbibliotheek, 49; Madrid, Bibliotheca Nacional 512. Our sincere thanks to the librarians.

TO FOLLOWERS OF THE RULE OF SAINT BENEDICT

Hinc celer egrediens facili, mea carta, volatu
per silvas, colles, valles quoque prepete cursu
alma deo cari Benedicti tecta require.
Est nam certa quies fessis venientibus illuc,
hic olus hospitibus, piscis hic, panis abundans;
pax pia, mens humilis, pulcra et concordia fratrum,
laus, amor et cultus Christi simul omnibus horis.

Across the hills and in the valley's shade,
    Alone the small script goes,
Seeking for Benedict's beloved roof,
    Where waits its sure repose.
They come and find, the tired travellers,
    Green herbs and ample bread,
Quiet and brothers' love and humbleness,
    Christ's peace on every head.

translation by Helen Waddell, *Mediaeval Latin Lyrics*

CONTENTS

Library of Congress Cataloging in Publication Data (Revised)

Gilbert, Abbot of Swineshead, Holland, Lincolnshire.
   Sermons on the Song of songs.

   (His The works of Gilbert of Hoyland; v. 1-)
(Cistercian fathers series : no. 14, 20, 26
   Bibliography:
   Includes index.
   1. Bible. O.T. Song of Solomon—Sermons.
I. Title. II. Series.
BS1485.G49   223'.9'066   77-23026
ISBN 0-87907-426-4

GILBERT OF HOYLAND

Volume Three

ON THE
SONG OF SONGS

SERMON 33
SPIRIT, POWER, MERCY, AND ALL GRACES

The bride is anointed with spirit, power, mercy, and all graces. 1. At Easter one should come to the tomb with spiritual ointments. 2. Anointing means a good conscience, fragrance a good reputation. 3. How ointments differ from perfume; the good works of virtue are insipid and displeasing without the unction of the Spirit. 4. How attractive is the unction of mercy! How ready Christ is to pardon! 5. Hope of mercy raises up the despondent; Christ's mercy is a model for pastors. 6. Ointments and ways of anointing are varied. 7–8. Ointments and their fragrance are distinguished. 9. Pride and tepidity make the prayer of the Pharisee malodorous.

THE FRAGRANCE OF YOUR OINTMENTS SURPASSES ALL PERFUMES.*[1]

Sg 4:10

This day of the Lord's Resurrection which we solemnly celebrate each year compels me to begin my sermon by returning to our discussion of the ointments. Today the women come with perfumes.* Nicodemus likewise comes 'bearing a mixture of myrrh and aloes weighing about a hundred pounds'.* Mary Magdalen herself 'anointed the body' of Jesus 'in anticipation of his burial'.* You see what important mysteries are celebrated in ointments. They are great mysteries and who is qualified to discuss them? Who will worthily discern

Mk 16:1

Jn 19:39
Mk 14:8. Miquel
154, n. 15.

the differences between the ointments and expound
their properties? Deliberation on this subject requires
a man of experience, not of opinions. Indeed it is not
easy for anyone to discuss these ointments unless his
teacher has been Unction in person.

Ps 44:8   Today the Lord was anointed 'with the oil of
gladness more than his fellows,'* yet not without his
fellows. For how does one share as a fellow, who does
not rejoice and make glad and does not rise to new
joy together with him who rises? This is indeed an
opportune time to discuss the ointments with you,
but a time much more opportune to be filled with
the fragrance of ointments. You demand a sermon of
me and I ask of you the fragrance of ointments. By
what right do you haunt the tomb of the Lord
Jesus with the holy women, if you bring to it no
spiritual ointment? Today the Lord's flesh was
Ps 108:24   gloriously changed thanks to the oil.* Does it not
seem fitting that our hearts should be changed and
transformed into the oil of the spirit, the oil of
Hb 1:9; Ps 44:8 exultation and gladness?*

I had begun a sermon about ointments and here
our discussion bogs down in oil. Now what has oil to
do with ointment? Not a little, and if oil is not the
same in every respect, oil approaches and resembles
ointment to some extent. For although oil is not
fragrant, it soothes; oil does not smell sweet but you
are well anointed with oil. Here however the Bridegroom extols not so much the unction as the fragrance
in the ointments of the bride. 'And the fragrance of
your ointments', he says, 'surpasses all perfume.'

2. Not every soul abounds in sweet-smelling
ointments, as that woman in the book of Kings says
to the prophet: there is 'in my house only a little oil
2 K 4:2   to anoint myself'.* This woman has no ointments
compounded of sweet-smelling spices but a little plain
oil for anointing. Mary Magdalen, a woman not of
the Law but of the Gospel, brings an ointment of
Mk 14:3; Jn 12:3 precious spikenard, not a little but a whole pound.*
And Simon himself is reproached by the Lord with
not having anointed his head even with oil, while she
Lk 7:46   poured ointment over his head.* Do you see how

ointments are preferred to oil, especially sweet-
smelling ointments? For in addition to fulfilling their
function of anointing, they anticipate it with some
blessing of spiritual fragrance.

Ointment indeed is more limited but its fragrance
circulates among many. Even though but one person
be anointed, he is not the only one to share its bouquet. The bouquet of the ointment is shared by all,
since it circulates among all. Therefore the anointing
is yours; its fragrance belongs to others as well as to
yourself. He is well anointed and fully fragrant, who
enjoys blessings in God's sight and shares blessings in
men's sight. 'Rejoice in the Lord always,' with Paul,
'and again I say rejoice; let your modesty be known
to all men.'* Apply the joy to ointments, men's   *Ph 4:4-5*
awareness of your modesty to its fragrance. Hear
how Paul himself speaks of awareness as fragrance.
'And everywhere He manifests the fragrance of our
awareness of Him.'*   *2 Co 2:14*

Good then is the ointment and good is its
fragrance, spiritual exultation in the Lord and its
modest manifestation, happiness and awareness. He is
well anointed whom the Lord delights in the happiness of his inner conscience and who is delighted in
the Lord; and his fragrance is sweet who with Paul
delights all men in everything he does and delights
them only in the Lord;* for in his modest demeanor,   *1 Co 10:33.*
discreet labor and learned speech, the ointments of   *Lam 18, n. 78.*
inward eagerness and grace yield their fragrance. He is
well anointed who glories in the Lord and his fragrance
is sweet through whom the Lord is glorified before
men. To the man himself who yields the fragrance of
the Lord, his own fragrance is sweet, if he does not
boast that he himself is praised but that the Lord is
praised through him.

3. 'The fragrance of your ointments surpasses all
perfumes.' Do you wish me to suggest for you the
difference between ointments and perfumes? Well
does this very text of the Canticle seem to make the
distinction not by depreciating perfumes but by
preferring ointments. As far then as I can find any
difference between similar and related substances,

ointments can be seen as gifts of grace conferred through the Holy Spirit,* while perfumes are our duties faithfully referred to the Holy Spirit.† In our tasks and duties exists the attractive beauty of natural goodness but in ointment exists the grace of the Spirit. You read that the Lord Jesus was 'anointed with spirit and virtue';* so also it was fitting that his bride should resemble him in this respect, that she also should be 'anointed with spirit and virtue'.

Good are the perfumes of the virtues and though they seem to have their own bouquet, they yield an aroma filled with more grace, when sprinkled with the 'fragrance of sweetness' from the unction of the Spirit.* The perfume of good works and virtues we can share in common with outsiders; ointments we cannot share in common. Scripturally, although virtues and good works are beautiful in themselves, they are more pleasing when they proceed from the Spirit. Why do men glorify God when they see good works, if not because they understand that the good work itself comes from God and returns to God?* Surely if there are any good works in me, they are more pleasing to me when they are ascribed to the grace of Christ,* when his unction in me is extolled and when the Spirit yields a sweet fragrance, than when my natural power of choice or the fruit of my industry is applauded.

Scripturally, without the unction of the Spirit nature is deprived of freedom, virtue of truth and work of merit.* For without the grace of the Spirit and faith in Christ, the effort of the will lacks effectiveness, what seems to be virtue is a veneer and the work does not reap a harvest of eternal reward. Therefore 'the fragrance of your ointments surpasses all perfumes'. For however varied their bouquet may be, these perfumes do not diffuse a fragrance of unadulterated sweetness, unless the anointing grace of the Spirit is diffused through them wave upon wave.

4. Do you wish me to set before you an ointment whose fragrance surpasses all other perfumes of the

Margin notes:

1 Jo 2:20, 27;
1 Co 12:4-11

†Col 3:12

Ac 10:38

2 Co 2:15; Ep 5:2;
Ph 4:18

Lk 23:47. See T4.

1 Co 15:10

See S 39:3-4

Church's gifts? In the Church what fragrance breathes a sweeter scent than that of mercy and forgiveness? How many have run in the fragrance of this ointment and through it been incorporated and engrafted in Christ! Sweet is its scent as it destroys in a moment the stench of inveterate corruption and of sin long ingrained.

How malodorous was that woman who was in the city, Mary by name, as she approached the feet of Jesus in the house of Simon the leper! How she stank in the nostrils of Simon himself, who could not endure the loathsomeness of her presence. How she stank, I say, as she approached Jesus! Yet notice how the fragrance of her repentance and love and of the grace she received is spread through the world! The grace of Christ does not delay; at the very banquet at which this woman bathed, wiped and anointed the Lord's feet, she is washed and wiped clean and fully anointed and preferred to the Pharisee by the witness of the Lord himself.* For the clemency of Christ is *Lk 7:37-50* neither niggardly nor indolent; it repays with interest and repays on the spot. What wonder if his pardon runs to meet the penitent, when his patience escorts her to repentance! Behold that woman taken in adultery and abandoned in the midst of all! Notice how she perfumed the air with the aroma of his clemency, though previously she reeked of the guilt of her wantonness.[2]

Thumb through the Gospel; everywhere you will find Jesus both quick and spendthrift in pardon. In John, although a man has been dead four days and now stinks according to the sad news published about him, when Jesus summons and leads him from the tomb of bad habit, when Jesus unbinds him and applies the ointment of forgiveness, on the spot there vanishes from his countenance all the stench of aging corruption.* Who indeed will re-examine a *Jo 11:1-44* charge not made by the Lord? Who will retain the errors which he remits?[3] That cannot be fetid which he fills with fragrance. 'Lord', said Martha, 'he has been dead four days and by now he stinks.'* Yours is *Jo 11:39* the error, Martha; Jesus does not take flight from what stinks, but rather sends the stench packing. He set the example for his Church, that as he did for us personally, so we also should do for one another.* These are the ointments he left to his Church.

Jo 13:15

5. How many in desperation would have given themselves up to all uncleanness and avarice,* and hurled themselves headlong into the whirlpool of all vices, if they had not been drawn back by the fragrance of this remedy! 'I would be distressed,' we chant, 'if I did not know the mercies of the Lord',[4] mercies in the Head and mercies in his Body which is the Church. For she also has received from the Lord what she hands on to her children.[5] She has received mercy in trust, I say, and in the command to her that she be the handmaid of mercies. Good it is to be mercy's servant, but better to be mercy's self.

Eph 4:19

The mercy you owe in virtue to your office, dispense from the heart. Manifest in yourself the affection of Christ whose office and place you have accepted. You are the minister of the One 'who is rich in mercy'.* Do not be found overharsh in what belongs to another. Distribute to your fellow servants[6] their measure of this ointment in good time. 'If you are unfaithful in what belongs to another, who will give you what is your own?'* Let your affection be one of mercy, for mercy is the result of the Lord's pardon. The man who nurses an injured conscience or a hidden wound[7] in his breast, will trust himself to you without anxiety if he scents in you the fragrance of this ointment. 'If you only knew what this means: "I desire mercy and not sacrifice", you would never have condemned the guiltless.'* Not so do you act, O Lord, not so! Not only do you not condemn the guiltless, but even the guilty you do not condemn but correct.

Eph 2:4

Lk 16:12

Mt 12:7

'The just man,' says the psalmist, 'shall correct me in mercy, but the oil of the wicked shall not anoint my head.'* Here the psalmist distinguishes between one oil and another, between the oil of flattery and the oil of mercy. The former soothes and wounds; the latter soothes and heals. Does not the ointment by which all sins are so easily blotted out have a sweeter

Ps 140:5

fragrance for you than all perfumes? That younger
son coming to his senses, even from a far off country,
perceived the rich supply of this ointment in his
father, and amid droves of hogs, the fragrance of his
father's clemency began to perfume the air. So the
son was allured and began to run to his father 'in the
fragrance of his ointments'.* See how accessible,   *Sg 1:3*
how overflowing is the grace of the Lord Jesus. He
finds it fitting to rejoice and feast with the repentant
son.* He stays in Zacchaeus' home;† he co-opts a   **Lk 15:11-32*
tax gatherer as his disciple** and with Lazarus   *†Lk 19:1-10*
straight from the tomb he celebrates a feast.††   ***Mt 9:9; 10:3*
He cannot reproach those to whom he is propitious;   *††Jo 12:1-2*
he does not know how to confer a half-measure of
clemency; those whom he forgives, he welcomes into
his familiar friendship.[8]

6. Good then is the ointment of mercy, because
it forgives sins, because it anticipates, accompanies
and accumulates merits. It surpasses the fragrance of
all perfumes, because the whole assembly of the
saints relies more on mercy than on merit. In James,
the ointment of forgiveness is the last Sacrament.*   *Jm 4:14-15*
This ointment is a blessing bestowed on sinner and
saint alike. But some other ointments are reserved
for the saints and suited to them alone. There are
ointments which heal, ointments which strengthen,
ointments which sanctify, ointments which give
delight. The first dispel sickness; the second add zest
to those who are already healthy; the third sanctify
for the work of the ministry, as royal and priestly
unctions sanctify; the fourth are intended not for
work but for leisure; not for administration but for
love, for glory, for delight, for the use of the Bridegroom and his bride.

It is good to linger among ointments, but since
enough has been said elsewhere about their various
kinds,* let us now briefly distinguish the various   *See Bernard,*
ways of anointing. Some persons are touched, others   *SC 10 ff.*
are sprinkled, others daubed, others steeped in ointments. Reread the Pentateuch, unroll the Gospel
again and make moral applications of the various
ways of anointing performed externally upon the

body. I am now concerned not with the nature of the ointments but with the measure of the anointing. Some persons receive ointments once, others often, others all the time. Good is this frequency, provided grace is also present. Neither sweetness nor plenty seems to be lacking in the bride's ointments, for 'their fragrance surpasses all perfumes'.

7. We have applied this eulogy to the Church in general; let us now direct the sermon to some specific person in the Church, one who through some singular gift of love and familiarity should be graced with the name of 'bride', one in whom the ointments not only of kinship but also of worthiness and charm perfume the air with rich fragrance. In my opinion such a person has neither been touched in some part nor sprinkled here and there with the sacred unction, but more bountifully steeped and wholly anointed in the delights of the Bridegroom. In the palace of this Bridegroom, ample storerooms are filled with perfumes, overflowing from room to room as befits the wealth of kings. But it is not beyond belief that the queen diffuses the fragrance of more excellent ointments. Yet nothing is told us about the effectiveness of the ointments beyond the fact that only their fragrance is extolled. The Bridegroom does not mention the effect of the anointing, being content to recall only their delights and preferably those delights which enkindle spiritual love.

Anointing is felt only by the sense of touch, when oil has been poured upon the flesh. But fragrance, eluding the sense of touch, allows itself to be experienced only in breathing. And while ointment liquefying gradually seeps downwards, its fragrance mounts upward unhindered, infiltrates the brain and while it occupies the seat of the senses, brings refreshment. The fragrance therefore of the ointments is much finer and more subtle than their fluid. And in the bride's wooing, it was fitting to mention what is more delicate, more adapted to spiritual delights and less cloyed with sediment. Other persons need ointments and oil either to allay or to transform the movements of the flesh. But the bride, as becomes the betrothed of the Lord, is now filled not in the flesh but in the spirit with delights of the spirit. 'The fragrance of your ointments surpasses all perfumes.'

Although only fragrance is mentioned, perhaps fragrance does not operate alone but anointing co-operates. 'Those who belong to Christ,' says the apostle, 'have crucified their flesh with its passions and desires.'* Where there is anointing, crucifixion seems unnecessary. The latter brings death while the former brings change. Crucifixion indeed inflicts pain, but anointing alleviates pain. Unction is gentle though effective, for without injury, by the oil of exultation and gladness,* unction keeps the flesh unharmed from corruption, banishes decay and inflicts no torment. Ointments anticipate and ointments follow the Passion of the Lord Jesus, that you also may learn to allay any possible torments of your flesh by an outpouring of abundant ointments. Twice was the Lord anointed, that he might not feel the insult and injury of the Cross and might achieve the renewal of his Resurrection, and that by his sacrament, as it were, he might commend the grace of spiritual anointing. Good then is the ointment when its flow, so to speak, transforms the flesh and when its fragrance refreshes the spirit.

8. To sum up in brief: anointing is an exultation of the mind and its fragrance is prayer. Anointing is spiritual gladness and its fragrance is some exterior awareness by reputation of what takes place in the spirit. Anointing is inward delight and its fragrance is a desire flowing gently from joyful experience. Therefore 'the fragrance of your ointments surpasses all perfumes'. Indeed the incense of every other prayer and desire is surpassed in vehemence[9] by that longing which is born from the wooing of heavenly joy and from the ardor, which like a most enchanting fragrance, rises in abundance from the anointing of the Spirit. Good is this longing which has the power of prayer without the distress of affliction.

She is the bride to whom this privilege of ointment and fragrance is accorded. What wonder if hers is a more excellent fragrance, when hers is a more

Ga 5:24

Ps 44:8; Hb 1:9

special anointing! What wonder if her hunger is
keener, when she savors what is sweeter! For it is
only right that she who clings more closely should
pray more fully. Clinging to the Bridegroom, she has

1 Co 6:17;
Lam 191, n. 141

been made one spirit with him.* Wherefore only
the Spirit yields his fragrance in her, for he has
anointed her and prays for her with affections too

Rm 8:26

deep for words.* Therefore 'the fragrance of her
ointments surpasses all perfumes'. Again in the
Apocalypse you read of 'bowls full of incense, which

Rv 5:8

are the prayers of the saints'.* Perfumes, as Exodus
teaches, are divided for two uses: namely for anoint-

Ex 25 and 30

ing and for the offering of incense.*

9. Do both these not seem to you to be combined now in the praise of the bride? Her ointments
are not only ointments but also most odoriferous, for
'their fragrance surpasses all perfumes'. Ointment, as
has been said, is the reception of gifts; fragrance is
thanksgiving for their reception, desire for eternal
gifts and a feeling of humility amid sublime blessings.
For 'the prayer of the man who humbles himself

Si 35:21.
Lam 188,
nn. 118, 121.

penetrates even the clouds'.* Do you see how the
incense of humble prayer ascends?

That Pharisee ascended into the Temple to pray
but the fragrance of his prayer knew not how to
ascend. He reviews for himself the gifts of graces
granted him by God and, as it were, enumerates
anointings. 'I am not', he says, 'like the rest of men,
extortioners, unjust, adulterers.' Do you hear at whose
expense he boasts that he has been anointed? His
glory is in the confusion of others. Though not
much to boast about, his glory seems much to him.
It smells sweet to him though not 'above perfumes'
but only above the nauseating fumes of 'the rest
of men'.

You have heard to what his anointings are preferred; hear now the elements of grace which his
ointments display, over which the Pharisee boasts:
'I fast twice a week, I give tithes of all I possess, and
if I have cheated anyone I make fourfold restitu-

Lk 18:11-12

tion.'* These good works reek of the rudiments of
the Law, not the perfection of the Gospel.[10] He

does not fast at all times, he does not renounce all his possessions, so as to have nothing from which to give the firstfruits or the tithes. He makes fourfold restitution when he has defrauded others, but he does not allow himself to be defrauded, does not offer what is left to one who takes away a part, does not say he has endured wrongdoing.* *Lk 6:29-30*

O Pharisee, amid feeble deeds you are boastful beyond measure![11] O Pharisee, you do not invoke God, but invoke insults on the tax collector hard by! You bear witness concerning yourself; your witness counts for little. Two faults in your prayer yield not so much a fragrance as a stench: pride and lukewarmness. The pride consists in your reproaching the tax collector, the lukewarmness in your asking for nothing at all. For how shall a prayer not be lukewarm which is filled with the bombast and the hollowness of self-adulation? O Pharisee, you do not praise God; you praise yourself! You bear witness concerning yourself and your witness is not true.* *Jo 5:31*
The evidence for your good work is slight; the evidence for preferring yourself to others is false.

Now listen to the witness of Truth: 'I tell you solemnly, the publican went down to his house justified rather than the other.'*[12] 'For it is not the *Lk 18:14*
man who commends himself who is accepted but the man whom the Lord commends.'* Happy then is the *2 Co 10:18*
soul for which such an excellent recommendation is given by Truth itself: 'The fragrance of your ointments surpasses all perfumes.' Great as was the evidence given for the tax collector, much greater witness is given to the bride for whom is sung the eulogy of our text. 'That man went down to his house justified rather than the Pharisee', that is rather than the proud man, the unjust man, but 'the fragrance of the bride's ointments surpasses all perfumes'. Here is a noble encomium, but she does not hear the witness of a man but of the One who searches hearts,* who by faith and love both dwells *Rv 2:23*
and works in her heart. She does not commend herself; she does not reproach others. Indeed 'her lips are a dripping honeycomb'.* This verse comes *Sg 4:11*

next but it cannot be dealt with today. Tomorrow's discourse will give your hearing and your eagerness, joy and gladness in the Lord Jesus. This may He grant who lives and reigns for ever and ever. Amen.

NOTES ON SERMON THIRTY-THREE

1.   G. writes to one individual, except in par. 1, the second sentence of par. 3 and the first sentence of par. 4.

2.   Jn 8:3-11. Lam 7, n. 14; 180, n. 63; for *evangelium revolve,* S 33:6, 34:1.

3.   Often G.'s reflections are redolent of the Prayers of St Anselm; Anselm asks, 'who will make excuse for him whom God accuses?' (Ward, 142, 1. 45) Here G. asks antiphonally: 'Who will re-examine a charge not made by the Lord? Who will retain the errors which he remits?' The originals show a closer link in sentence structure.

4.   In the Cistercian and Roman Breviaries, this is the responsory to lesson VII, nocturn II of Vigils for the First Sunday of Lent.

5.   1 Co 11:23. See A. Ampe, 'Exemplarisme,' DSp 4 (1961) 1877.

6.   Reading *conservis* with mss Paris 9605, 8546, Bruges 49, Madrid 512, Mab, for *conversis* of Migne.

7.   Reading *caecum* of Paris 9605, 8546, Bruges 49, Madrid 512, for *tectum* of Mab. and Migne.

8.   On *familiaritas,* see S 33:5, 7; 44:2; 45:3; 46:3; Lam 187, n. 114.

9.   Reading *vehementiam* with mss Paris 9605, 8546, Bruges 49, Madrid 512, Migne, for *vehementia* of Mab. On the joy of experience see Miquel 157-8, n. 28; Lam 192, n. 149.

10.   Reading *perfectionem* with mss Paris 9605, 8546, Bruges 49, Troyes 917, for *doctrinam* of Madrid 512, Mab. and Migne.

11.   With mss Paris 9605, 8546, Bruges 49, Madrid 512, Troyes 917, Mab. and Migne reading *infirma* rather than the suggested *infima*.

12.   G. begins his quotation with 'Amen, Amen' as if from Jn.

SERMON 34
WORKS, LIPS AND SPIRIT

The bride pleases in .works, lips and spirit.
1. From the Bridegroom through the Spirit
comes the rank of ministry and the grace to
minister. 2. The bride's lips are compared to a
honeycomb because they distill the sweetness
of the fourfold works of his word. 3. Sweet is
her pardon and her prayer. 4. Her lips are a
honeycomb thanks to the kiss of charity and
the utterance of truth. 5. She distills the honey
of mysteries and pours with discretion the
milk of consolation. 6. Her cloak of strength is
in fasting and incense is in her prayer. 7. The
garment of good deeds and the raiment of the
flesh lend charm to her body and win grace for
her soul. 8. The bride pleases her Bridegroom
in words, works, and the Spirit.

YOUR LIPS ARE A DRIPPING HONEYCOMB, MY
BRIDE: HONEY AND MILK ARE BENEATH YOUR
TONGUE: THE FRAGRANCE OF YOUR GAR-
MENTS IS LIKE THE FRAGRANCE OF INCENSE*[1]   *Sg 4:11*

Passionately tender are the words now addressed to the bride. But you ask how they relate to what precedes. Once should have been enough to remind you that the law of eulogy is free from the obligation of logical sequence.* It does not follow a chain but enjoys   *G. S 1:1*
freedom to wander. Where the logic of praise is concerned, order cannot indeed be demanded, but it

should not be brushed aside if it can be identified.
Immediately after the eulogy of ointments, the grace
of her lips is introduced. Have you any reason to
doubt that through the power of the ointment this

Ps 44:3 grace was diffused upon her lips?* Consult the
Gospel and you will find a similar remark about the
Bridegroom himself: 'The Spirit of the Lord,' he
says, 'is upon me, because he has anointed me; he

Lk 4:18 sent me to preach good news to the poor.'*

Fittingly the bride was likened to the Bridegroom,
in being also anointed for the work of the Gospel by
the unction of the Spirit. For the Spirit anoints both
for office and for effectiveness. Both come from
him: the rank of ministry and the grace to minister.
Without grace the rank is useless and without rank
the exercise of grace is presumptuous. 'How shall
they preach, if they are not sent, unless they are

Rm 10:15 anointed?'* As it was written, 'The Spirit of the
Lord . . . has anointed me; he has sent me to preach

Lk 4:18 good news to the poor.'* The Spirit ordains to
office. The Spirit both opens the mouth and teaches
it to speak. Therefore in the eulogy of the bride, the
Bridegroom deals first with ointments and then with
the sweetness of her lips, for although she utters a
gentle message, she is not the speaker, but the Spirit
of the Bridegroom speaks in her. In the Gospel, listen
to what the Bridegroom himself, Jesus, promises to
his pristine bride, that is, to the apostles who received
the firstfruits of the Spirit: 'I will give you a mouth
and wisdom,' he says, 'which none of your adversaries

Lk 21:15 will be able to withstand or contradict.* Great
indeed is the power of God's word; it can both refute
adversaries and win those who are not adversaries.

Now the Lord's promise concerns the preaching
of the word; but what is central to our discussion, his
promise, looks more to persuasion than to the effectiveness of refutation: 'Your lips are a dripping
honeycomb.' It is a family trait and, as it were, inborn
in her to speak sweetly. But if ever she gives a severe
rebuke it is foreign to her, imported from afar and
not inherent in her; if she rebukes, it is not from disposition but under duress. When she speaks sweetly,

she speaks in character, but when harshly, what provokes her is not the temper of her tongue but the distemper of her audience. Therefore, for what is a family trait and in character, the Bridegroom praises her in the words: 'Your lips are a dripping honeycomb.'

2. Since you have now heard something about the link with what precedes, do you wish me to expand upon the content of this eulogy? The eulogy contains three points: sweetness, fulness, and thrift. The sweetness of the honeycomb is considered in its quality, fulness in its abundance, thrift in its outpouring. Why do I say outpouring? It is rather a distillation than an outpouring, for 'your lips are a dripping honeycomb'. Why need we linger to give each point its application? You know yourselves that a honeycomb pours out only sweetness and pours sweetness only from a full comb and indeed pours some but not all its fulness. Therefore 'your lips are' not an outpouring but 'a dripping honeycomb'. On the lips of the bride then is only sweetness and full sweetness and measured sweetness. Sweetness is indeed fully possessed, yet poured not fully but exactly as the capacity of the audience requires.

Do you also wish to hear the evidence from the very lips of the bride herself? 'How sweet are your words to my taste, sweeter than honey to my mouth.'*[2] Sweet indeed are the lips of the bride   *Ps 118:103* for the sayings of the Lord distill from her lips. This sweetness belongs to the sayings of the Lord. Indeed she does not speak on her own, but, as it were, delivers the messages of the Lord; therefore grace is poured upon her lips.* Hear now in part what kinds   *Ps 44:33* of honey the comb of the divine word distills and what amount God has allotted for each vessel into which honey is distilled.

The honeycomb of the divine word remits and permits, promises and prepares. It remits sins, permits infirmities, promises eternal blessings and prepares in advance some firstfruits of those blessings. It speaks wisdom among the perfect, wisdom indeed not of this world but God's wisdom hidden in

1 Co 2:7   mystery,* and among those less spiritually wise it
considers that it 'knows nothing but Christ Jesus and
1 Co 2:2   him crucified'.* His word encourages us toward perfection, it does not compel; still more, it consoles
the fainthearted, bears up the weak and, if it corrects
the restless, the correction itself has the taste of
1 Th 5:14   maternal sweetness.* His word has compassion on the
sinner; it pardons the converted; it sets no measure or
limit to its pardon beyond which it may not go, for
we are commanded to forgive seventy times seven
times a day one who confesses his sins that many
Mt 18:22   times.*

3.   See what a great store of sweetness is on the
Heb 2:1   lips of the bride, who as often as you drift into evil,*
if you be converted, so often drips honey into you
for your good and is not exhausted by her role of
pardoner. In Luke, like the angels of God she does not
Lk 15:10   insult but instead exults over one repentant sinner.*
Good then it is to lend a hearing to her lips. Indeed
even the Lord bends his ear to her prayers and so
challenges and invites your affection that he even
betrays his own. Say what you have to say, O bride,
for your Beloved listens eagerly whether you speak
about him or whether you chat with him. But when
the bride speaks with the Bridegroom himself, then
she speaks with a sweeter song on her lips and she
speaks with another tongue. Then the lips of her
heart truly distill a honey of divine delight, or rather
they do not so much distill as overflow, since at that
hour her whole soul is changed into honeyed affections.

Blessed is the exchange, when from the heart of
the bride some streams of honey flow into the
Beloved and from him return in waves to the bride.
Indeed to the source whence these rivers of honey
emerge they are restored that they may continue to
flow. Good are the honeycombs on the lips of Bridegroom and bride, rising from well-spring to well-
spring and sharing with each other the dews of love's
sweetness. He from on high drops down dews of
Gn 27:39   grace;* she from below returns the dew of thanksgiving. Jesus himself has begotten the drops of this

honeyed dew in the beloved soul. Wholly sweet are
these drops of dew, the affections of divine love,
when the bride is wholly dissolved into honeyed
drops before the face of the One she loves, before
the face of her God. Therefore her 'lips are like a
dripping honeycomb', because passionately sweet is
the ardor of a mind so affectionate; but the ardor is
quickly cut short, because that rapture of the mind
is sweet to excess and because all too soon it is
interrupted.

4. 'Your lips are a dripping honeycomb.' I consider these lips entirely purified, for from them Jesus
himself recalls that he draws honeyed sweetness.
Isaiah's lips were purified by being touched with
tongs and a coal from the altar.* 'The Lord put   *Is 6:6-7*
forth his hand,' says Jeremiah, 'and touched my
mouth.'*³ One who is a bride desires not a coal, not a   *Jr 1:9*
finger, but the touch of his lips. 'Let him kiss me,'
she says, 'with the kiss of his mouth.'* Lips cry for   *Sg 1:1*
lips. Nor indeed would sweetness be pressed from
the bride's lips, if her lips did not receive the impress
of her Beloved's lips. Yet in what else does he rejoice
but in the sweetness of the kiss, which he steals from
the bride's lips, when he says: 'Your lips are a dripping
honeycomb'? Thanks to both, thanks to the kiss of
charity and thanks to the utterance of truth, he says:
'Your lips are a dripping honeycomb; honey and milk
are beneath your tongue.'

Milk beneath the tongue refers properly to the
grace of speech. The lips are also used for a kiss but
the tongue only for speech. Not only does sweetness
ring upon the tongue but 'milk and honey are beneath your tongue'. Sweetness which is counterfeit
rings only upon the tongue and is not tasted beneath
the tongue. Slight is the sweetness, which is wholly on
the lips and on the tongue and whose greater part is
not beneath the tongue. Sweetness is not only on the
bride's tongue or wholly on her tongue, but as he who
knows bears witness: 'Milk and honey are beneath
your tongue'. Therefore, she breaks out in a goodly
word, a word both of honey and of milk, thanks
to the majesty of his Godhead and thanks to the

mystery of his Incarnation. Her tongue and her lips are like a silver channel through which streams of milk and honey bubble from the fountain of her heart. Each is sweet but their sweetness is different: milk is for babes, as Paul says,* while he also teaches a sweet and divine and, as it were, a honeyed wisdom for the perfect.*[4]

5. Some people have only honey beneath their tongues and no milk, others only milk and no honey. But beneath the bride's tongue are both alike, honey and milk. The bride does not pour but rather distills the honey; neither indeed does she pour at random and without restraint those sublime and hidden senses of heavenly secrets and the mysteries of the Godhead, nor does she give milk to drink without discretion. 'Honey and milk are beneath your tongue', says the Bridegroom. Indeed her message is neither devoid of inner sweetness nor equal to her own inner sweetness. A sweet message is on the tip of her tongue for 'beneath her tongue are honey and milk'.

Blessed is the tongue which distills like a honeycomb and is distended like breasts with milk for babes, which distills honey and flows with milk. All outcry, bitterness and blasphemy are banished far from these lips according to the persuasive warning of Paul.* Nor are 'fraud and oppression beneath her tongue' in the words of the Psalm,* but 'honey and milk are beneath your tongue' in the words of the Bridegroom. 'A dripping honeycomb are the lips of the harlot,' says the book of Proverbs 'and her throat is smoother than oil.' Yet neither milk nor honey is beneath her tongue, neither in her hidden way nor in her final day, 'but in the end she is bitter as wormwood, sharp as a two-edged sword'.*

Yet of the valiant woman the same book of Proverbs says: 'Strength and beauty are her clothing and she will laugh on the last day.'* Even now her mouth gives birth to that spiritual and really happy laughter and its sweetness, as it were, 'lies hidden beneath her tongue'. But the milk and honey which now lie under her tongue will bubble up into full happiness on the last day. Then joy will nowise be

1 Co 3:1-2

1 Co 2:6

Eph 4:31
Ps 10:7

Pr 5:3-4

Pr 31:25

choked in silence beneath the tongue, but long
suppressed it will burst out and fill her mouth with
laughter,* the mouth of the woman, I repeat, 'whose   *Jb 8:21*
clothing is strength and beauty'. Notice how im-
proper it is for her to be discovered stripped of her
clothing, who expects the promised joys to be
given her.

6. Who knows whether these are not the same
garments mentioned in the same verse of our Canticle: 'the fragrance of your garments is like the
fragrance of incense'? 'I clothed my soul in fasting,'
says the psalmist,* and again I shall 'humble my soul   *Ps 68:11*
in fasting and my prayer will be folded back on my
bosom'.* Fasting is a good garment and in its hidden   *Ps 34:13*
bosom, as it were, prayer dwells. It is a garment with a
fold like a bosom: 'My prayer shall be folded back on
my bosom.' Here you have both, if you notice: in
fasting, the cloak of strength; and in prayer, the
fragrance of incense. 'My prayer shall be folded back
on my bosom.'

Why then does he say 'on my bosom?' Does he
wish us to understand perhaps the failure of lukewarm
and interrupted prayer, vanishing in the very first
upward motion? Is prayer then said to be 'folded
back on its bosom', that is, to relapse into the
very place whence it rose? But how is what perishes
folded back and returned? That prayer seems rather
to be 'folded back on its bosom' which quickly
though not fully obtains what it seeks; at least in part
it receives the reward of a humble and devout
petition. Prayer, importunate and devout, has indeed
much sweetness. While prayer rises in the sight of the
Lord like incense,* it breathes in the sweet scent of   *Ps 140:2.*
its own fragrance. Is that not a good cloak, when the   *Lam 188, n. 118*
mist from such a cloud enfolds and invests the very
soul of the suppliant? A good cloak it is, but as we
have begun, so let us continue our interpretation of
the garments in terms of outward actions.

7. Now good deeds both cover previous deform-
ity, lest it be charged to our loss, and lend some
beauty and charm that it may be counted as gain.
Good garments then are the good deeds which

both grace the body and win grace for the soul. That
they grace the body is obvious but not everyone's
finery yields the fragrance of incense and displays a
pattern of prayer. According to Scripture, when
anyone's deeds, powerful for all to see,[5] smack of
ostentation and vainglory,* not of insistent supplication, not of eagerness to please the Lord,* not of
desires to win grace, how shall the scent of such a
one's finery be compared to 'the fragrance of
incense'?

Est 1:4

1 Co 7:32;
2 Co 11:28

But when a man does everything in order to please
God with whom he enlisted* and to deserve his favor,
certainly 'the fragrance of his garments is like the
fragrance of incense'. Incense is wont to be offered
and ought to be offered only to God; therefore 'the
fragrance of his garments is like the fragrance of
incense', since whatever he does whether openly or
secretly is directed to obtaining divine propitiation.
Oil in vessels seems to be the same as fragrance in
garments, if it is the fragrance of incense. For what
else but those spiritual joys and eternal delight
does one ask of God, when one renounces and abhors
all other delight?

2 Tm 2:4

'My soul thirsts for you,' says the Psalm, 'in how
many ways does my flesh thirst for you!'* You see in
these words how the very garment of the flesh plays
the role of prayer, when the flesh is said to thirst for
God. Does not the flesh which is afflicted by voluntary mortification strive to bend God to propitiation?
The very sufferings of the flesh on God's account are
supplications to him. Alms given in compassion to
the poor implore him; why should the discreet
curbing of one's own bodily pleasures not be as
effective as prayer? The curbing of pleasure is an expression of one's yearnings and of a desire which
sighs for a different delight. The result of fervent
prayer returns and 'folds back upon the bosom of the
heart'. Incense yields a sweet fragrance in the garment
of outward abstinence.

Ps 62:2.
Lam 192, n. 146.

Wholly good is the garment, when the soul is
robed not so much in the flesh as in a chastening fast
from pleasures of the flesh. Wholly good is the

garment of virginal continence; like incense it wafts a sweet fragrance to him who is loved and to her who loves. Whatever is offered with love, she who makes the offering cannot fail to enjoy its delight. Indeed all this sweetness which is commended in her is also perceived by herself. From her it flows and in her it remains. On her lips is a honeycomb, beneath her tongue honey and in her garments the scent of incense. Closest to herself are these three gifts so pleasing to the senses, so sweet to enjoy. 'The words of my mouth will be pleasing,' says David, 'and the meditation of my heart ever in your sight.'* Here you have each of two gifts, and that nothing may be wanting to the fulness of grace, by the mention of 'garments' in the third place, is inserted the quality of good deeds. From the lips words drop; beneath the tongue flow honeyed meditations; the adornment of garments wafts the fragrance of incense.

Ps 18:15.
Lam 186, n. 105.

8. What do you think is absent from her glory, when in her these three gifts are equally pleasing: her lips, her spirit and her work? In this number all are included but reversed in their order. Indeed one must begin with works, not with words. The works and prayers of Cornelius the centurion were heard first. By faith their hearts were cleansed and then the Spirit descended upon him and his household and they spoke with tongues.* The apostles themselves after the Ascension of the Lord with one accord persevered in prayer;* then when the days assigned for the promise were complete they were filled with the Spirit,* and afterwards they set out and preached everywhere.* First was their prayer in profusion, then an infusion of the Spirit; so the grace they acquired, they poured in profusion for others. First in expectation and longing they were turned towards God; secondly God turned towards them; thirdly, once turned to God, they form and strengthen their brethren in his likeness.*

Ac 10:2, 46.

Ac 1:14

Ac 2:4
Mk 16:20

Lk 22:32;
Rm 8:29

But whether you consider holiness of life in the apostles, God's visitation, or their ministry of the word,* all these take the place of garments, with all these they were covered and adorned. In them what

Ac 20:24

was left naked or shabby with its original stains, when they were brilliantly vested in the gay raiment of the word and of virtue? Splendid then was their raiment but not less was their influence. What perfume pours from their garments? What kind of fragrance have they? Is it not 'the fragrance of incense'? When they distribute their Lord's money to fellow servants, they do not allow a bit of it to remain with themselves even unobserved; they do not fraudently filch a coin for themselves. They shake their hands loose even from the tribute of praise,* attributing everything to the glory of God. Like the heavens they have been robed in beautiful light, but like the heavens they proclaim not their own glory but the glory of God.*

Is 33:15

Ps 18:1

Paul himself by his words wove for you some delicate and incorruptible garments and according to your measure he fits you with a mantle of light and understanding, yet not in the plausible 'words of human wisdom but in the teaching of the Spirit'.* Therefore both the garments, with which he is covered himself and which he has woven for you, have the fragrance only of incense. An affected display of words seems to reek of the affectation of idle foppery and vanity. Those again who pursue not the charm of eloquence but hazardous and fallacious argumentation on recondite subjects, while they expend themselves unduly for an empty fame, sometimes weave in patches of blasphemy.[6] So the fragrance of such a man's garments is not 'the fragrance of incense'. But not one of the bride's garments does the Bridegroom seem to exclude, since he commends without restriction: 'the fragrance of your garments is like the fragrance of incense'. Oh happy were I if even one or other garment upon me should yield the pure fragrance of incense, not spoiled by any foreign admixture! Indeed no one in my opinion has reached that stature where his whole wardrobe wafts the fragrance of incense, if he has not yet been found worthy to be elevated to the state of his brides by the Lord Jesus, the Bridegroom of brides.

1 Co 2:13

NOTES ON SERMON THIRTY-FOUR

1.   G. writes for one individual, except in two early sentences of par. 1, and in the first half of par. 2. See à Lapide, 8:72.
2.   See de Lubac, *Exégèse Médiéval,* 1:615, n. 13.
3.   See Bernard, SC 1-8; Gilbert uses 'embrace' more often.
4.   See De Lubac, *Exégèse Médiéval,* 1:612.
5.   Reading *potentia* with mss Paris 9605, 8546, Bruges 49, Madrid 512, Troyes 917, rather than *patentia* of Mab. or *patientia* of Migne.
6.   See Horace's purple patch, *Ars Poetica,* lines 14-16.

SERMON 35
FRUITS OF THE FOUNTAIN
AND THE GARDEN

From the fountain in the garden the bride
offers rich fruits. 1. The garden means interior
delights and the enclosure means the discipline
of standing watch. 2. Horticulture is useless
without custody; Adam was a hapless guardian;
we need custody for our spiritual garden.
3. This garden has a threefold praise; devotion
inspires the heart and makes the seeds of virtue
germinate. 4. A fountain constantly wells up
and when sealed is not drained away; as the
fountain is sealed with figures, the book is
wrapped in riddles. 5. Like paradise is the
conscience and behavior of the bride. 6. The
pomegranate shows the kinship of modesty and
patience. 7. Religious congregations are
likened to pomegranates.

A GARDEN ENCLOSED ARE YOU, SISTER, MY
BRIDE, A GARDEN ENCLOSED, A FOUNTAIN
SEALED. YOUR SPRAYS ARE A PARADISE OF
POMEGRANATES, WITH THE CHOICEST OF
FRUITS, . . . *[1]

Sg 4:12-13

Agarden are you, sister, my bride, a garden
enclosed, a fountain sealed.' From his words,
weigh first the affection of this panegyrist.
He seems delighted, since he is not content
with one eulogy. How great his affection would have
been, if without repetition he had spoken a simple
eulogy of the lady he addresses! Now however he

adopts recherché terms of courtesy and in tribute
doubles his compliments. Why should he not? Will
he not doubly rejoice in the precious endowments of
the one he chose for the grace of matrimony? Only
one who was worthy could be chosen for the
privileges of such sweet intimacy, nor once chosen
could she be loved lukewarmly. Is it not right that
she also should strive to please him in such privileges,
since he has given her such praise? He praises her, he
prepares her to match his praise, he plants her for
himself as a paradise of pleasure. He who personally
prepares her to match his praise, personally compares her to a paradise of delights.

'Behold,' said Isaac, 'the fragrance of my son is
like the fragrance of a bountiful field, which the Lord
has blessed.'* Yet his bride is compared not to a
field but to a garden, for there the planting of
flowers seems spiritual and the cultivation of spices
more bountiful. Into this garden, good Jesus, you
readily descend to the beds of spices, to recline in this
garden, to be its gardener and its guardian. 'A
garden enclosed,' he says, 'sister, my bride, a garden
enclosed.' Take the garden, brethren, to mean interior delights and the enclosure the discipline of
standing watch. Whom will you liken to a garden, but
one whose soul is as quickened with the scent of
spiritual affections as a garden with perfumed flowers?
What a pleasant sanctuary,[2] what a sweet retreat in
the bride's breast, a breast so luxuriant with flowers
that it is compared to a garden!

There no 'root of bitterness springing up',* chokes
the delights of this garden. 'Every plant which my
heavenly Father has not planted'* will not be found
in it. In Scripture, he himself planted this pleasure
garden, that he alone might cultivate and guard it.*
He cultivates it in two ways, by planting and by
weeding. He plants it that every seed may be true to
him, but he weeds it 'that it may bear more fruit'.* It
is planted that the seed may be true and it is
weeded that it may not be half empty. What is the
point of planting for truth, if failure to weed does
not provide abundance? The diligent cultivation of

Gn 27:27.
Lam 19, n. 83.

Heb 12:15

Mt 15:13

Gn 2:8, 15

Jr 2:21; Jn 15:2

discipline yields nothing without watch and ward. He lacks neither, who is likened to a garden and to a 'garden enclosed'.

2. 'A garden enclosed are you, sister, my bride.' Over the garden in which he was placed, Adam kept a poor watch against the slithering entry of the wily serpent. Pleasant indeed was that paradise of material trees, but I envisage a much fairer paradise planted in Adam's spirit. The serpent would have invaded that material garden harmlessly, if it had not squirmed into the garden of the spirit. The snake was welcomed and at once Adam felt deeply its venom, for 'a snake will bite someone who breaches a wall'.* A wall is a good protection, for a wall separates and keeps unharmed what is cultivated from what is not. Surround your garden then with this wall, lest, if the wall be removed and its cement crumbled, you become exposed to plunder and trampling. *Qo 10:8*

Adam's garden was not closed to his enemy but thereafter how heavily it was barred to Adam the outcast and exile! With no ease does Adam reenter the garden, from which with careless ease he fell.* In the sweat of his brow does he eat bread, who in paradise at will plucked fruit from the tree of life.* Here he eats his bread, there the fruits of life. In paradise 'the Lord . . . brought forth every tree fair to look upon and delicious to eat'.* Adam the outcast digs in the earth; not the Lord but the earth itself yields thorns and thistles for its cultivator. Paradise yields its fruit without labor but the earth fails to yield despite the laborer. It is a pitiful change but 'you destroy', O Lord, and justly, every 'unfaithful fornicator'.* Rightly is he destroyed, who by fornication destroys such intimate bonds and no longer deserves to hear such terms of endearment as the words 'sister', 'bride', 'garden' and 'garden enclosed', which admits none but the Beloved. *Heb 6:6* *Gn 3:2* *Gn 2:9* *Ps 72:27*

Let the door of your paradise be ever closed but opened only to your Prince. Let its panels not be 'broken down with hammer and hatchet'.* There let one entrance be built and this entrusted to the Cherubim. Let nothing be admitted which has not *Ps 73:6*

first been tested by their 'flaming sword', nothing
which the word of God may reject, which charity
may not approve, which may not approach the per-
Gn 3:24; 1 Co
1:19; Col 3:14;
Rm 13:10.
fection and 'fulness of the law'.* So the Cherubim
are fulness of knowledge and charity is the fulness of
the law; in charity are included all the command-
Si 1:20; Rm 13:10;
Mt 22:39; 40.
ments.* Let charity be for you a flaming guard, to
consume at once without delay anything unworthy
which attempts to break in. Is enclosure not aptly
attributed to love, which always controls the feelings
of the bride and encloses them in Love Itself, ever
turning her inwards where her delights may be to
Pr 8:31
dwell with the Son of God?*

A good wall is love but this wall has a rampart in
front of it. Love is like a wall and its rampart is the
strictness of the Rule. The wall encloses holy
thoughts and sweet affections; the rampart repulses
and shuts out occasions of sin. The rampart of the
Rule affords the opportunity of leisure for the
attentions of love; the wall of love enjoys them.[3]
The inner wall is pleasing; the outer rampart is
necessary. The wall encloses you amid heavenly
delights; the rampart excludes worldly pleasures. If it
is your desire to offer your heart to Christ as a garden
of delights, do not take it ill if you are enclosed by
this rampart. Anyone who complains of a bulwark
wishes to lose the delights he possesses, if indeed he
does possess them. One who knows not how to be
enclosed, knows not how to be a garden.

3. 'A garden enclosed, a fountain sealed. Your
sprays are a paradise of pomegranates, with the
choicest of fruits.' The Bridegroom completes the
praises of this garden in three points: it is enclosed
and watered and perfumed. Enclosure confers freedom from care; irrigation adds fruitfulness; perfume
concerns both the products of the garden and their
charm. Does this garden not seem charming to us, so
replete, so rich and so useful? Not only is the garden
useful, but it also abounds in perfumed delights. Who
among us would dare to attribute these praises to himself? Who would assume that these compliments are for

himself? As we appreciate the irrigation and germina-
tion of spices, so would that we did not depreciate
the enclosure and the seal. Indeed only a garden
enclosed and irrigated by the streams of a sealed
fountain produces these sprays of spices. Let your
fountain then be sealed, that it may not be totally
dried up by reckless outpouring; let it be sealed, that
it may satisfy your need for irrigation.

'Distribute your streams through your squares;
keep them to yourself, that strangers may not be
your partners.'* In the squares, I say, but in your   Pr 5:16
own squares, distribute your waters, that the spices
of the virtues may grow for you as if by the water in
the squares.* How shall he not be a fountain sealed,   Rv 22:2
who flows from that fountain of life which 'God the
Father sealed'?* Whoever will drink of this water   Jn 6:27
which I give, says the Lord, 'it will become in him a
spring of water welling up to eternal life'.* In this   Jn 4:13-14
fountain which the Beloved describes as 'sealed',
understand a teaching that is sealed and spiritual and
personal and withdrawn from the world—yes, either
a teaching or certainly a devotion, sealed with the
privilege of sweetness and, as it were, especially one's
own, flowing abundantly and continuously. This is
the fountain which creates all the joyful fruits of the
virtues. This is the stimulant for valiant deeds, like
marrow for their bones.* For this joy, this personal   Pr 3:8
and peerless devotion to God, refreshes the countenance of the heart.* It is like a sealed fountain of   Pr 15:13
one's own set apart for this service:* to water the   Rm 1:1
heart of the bride, who is like a garden meant for the
delights of the Bridegroom.

Let the fountain then be sealed, lest it become in
the words of Proverbs 'your spring muddied by the
foot, a polluted fountain'.* Otherwise your Beloved   Pr 25:6
knows not how to drink from a pure fountain. 'The
light of your countenance, O Lord,' says the psalmist,
'has been sealed upon us; you have given joy to my
heart.'* Apply the rejoicing to irrigation. In Psalms,   Ps 4:7
the garden germinating shall rejoice in the rivulets
from the fountain.* Do you not recall how in   Ps 64:11
Genesis a fountain began to rise and to water the

Gn 2:6
the whole surface of the earth?* The earth still gave
only its fruits; it was not yet acquainted with thorns
and thistles. Who will give this water to my little
garden and this fountain sealed to my flower beds?
Who will grant that the whole surface of my little
garden may be watered with rivulets of delight and
of light, that nothing in it may either be barren or
saddened by lack of devotion? Cheerless activity,
deprived of the irrigation of spiritual joy, seems close
to barrenness. In the words of Scripture, even if
something sprouts, it grows 'like a root from parched
Is 53:2
land'.* Like a root it is, not like flowers, not like
fruit; like a root, with little or nothing more than
a root.

4. The fountain was introduced to encourage
your belief that flourishing plants spring up in a
watered garden. There exists indeed a garden, whose
waters come by chance and, as it were, are imported
from without, not perennial, not part of the garden.
Good is the garden, however, when its fountain rises
from within. A fountain sealed and belonging to the
garden, as the Bridegroom says, is 'a fountain' and a
'fountain sealed', that is, constantly welling up from
within and unable to be polluted. 'A fountain'
because it flows in abundance; 'sealed' because nowhere is it drained away. Or perhaps hers is called 'a
sealed fountain' because, while others have other
fountains, for his sister and bride there exists a special
fountain of her own, one sealed by some particular
privilege.

Si 1:5; Pr 18:4
Entirely good is the fountain of wisdom,* but it
still flows to us beneath a seal; its taste is delicious
but it is not yet sparklingly clear for us. It is sealed
and enclosed in figures. In the Apocalypse, a book
sealed with seven seals is displayed in the hand of
Rv 5:1
'one seated upon a throne'.* The meaning of each,
both of the fountain and of the book, points to the
understanding of wisdom; but each is sealed with
figures and wrapped in riddles. Each is sealed but
through each wisdom is channelled to us through
disclosures and hidden from us in the same disclosures. As in the Apocalypse you read of the

openings of the sealed book, so here also you read of
the sprays of the sealed fountain.[4] 'Your sprays are a
paradise of pomegranates with the choicest of fruits.'
This fountain is indeed sealed but not dried up, since
its sprays are so full of grace. Sealed is the fountain of
wisdom but by its sprays you shall know it.

'There shall be a fountain opened for the House of
David,' says Zechariah, 'to cleanse them from sin and
from uncleanness.'* That fountain is open but this is   *Zc 13:1*
sealed; that washes away but this washes in. That
fountain cleanses but this irrigates. That purifies from
sins but this produces delights. That fountain is shared
by many but this is reserved for the bride. In Zechariah's fountain is remission of sins, in the bride's the
emission of sprays. In a psalm for the octachord, see
how first the psalmist floods his bed with tears, then
drenches his couch with weeping,[5] for it is not enough
to be scoured from filth unless fruitfulness follows
after.

5. 'Your sprays are a paradise of pomegranates.'
*Yes, good Jesus, this is so. These sprays are your
inspiration, inspirations channelled through good
angels. The fountain could not spray such delights,
unless you from within channelled the delights of
living water. 'The light of your countenance, O Lord,
has been sealed upon us; you have given joy to my
heart.'** That has been sealed upon us which has   *Ps 4:7*
been impressed upon us from on high. When the
image of the divine light from on high is impressed
upon anyone, abundance of spiritual joy is expressed
deep within the heart. Therefore the glorious sprays
of the king's daughter are from deep within. 'Your
sprays are a paradise.'* Not slender are the stores of   *Sg 4:13*
delights within, when from them sprouts a whole
paradise.

You have both, a paradise enclosed and a paradise
produced. The former exists in affections of purity;
the latter in acts of piety. Pure affection is within and
pious action proceeds from it and tests it. Each is
delightful: both the conscience and the behavior of
the bride. For she both proposes all things usefully
and disposes them well.* Accordingly you may see,   *Ws 8:1; 1 Tm 4:6*

as it were, a paradise in her outward demeanor and activity; her integrity makes her pleasing in each single action, her order when her actions are compared and her charm when her actions are summed up. She does everything with moderation and calm, that the serenity of virginal modesty in her may not be ruffled. In the Canticle, the Bridegroom, intending to list the blessings of this paradise, begins with modesty, proposing pomegranates as its symbol, thanks to their likeness in color. 'Your sprays are a paradise of pomegranates.'

6. Pomegranates can also be understood as the patience of the martyrs, because they have been stained red by their own blood. Yes, patience is a good companion to modesty; they are combined by James in the praise of wisdom: 'The wisdom from above is first pure, then peaceful.'* Modesty controls itself decorously and according to its rank, while patience bears with equanimity a lack of restraint in others. Modesty sets the style for its own actions; patience is a shield against the attacks of others. The one is style, the other strength. Therefore in Proverbs it is said: 'Strength and beauty are her clothing.'* 'It is first pure,' said James, 'then peaceful', and after a few words he adds, full of good works.* Good indeed it is to suffer persecution but for the fruits of justice.* Hence her sprays are pomegranates but with the choicest of fruits. Good indeed is modesty provided it be not idle, not affected, not hypocritical, but bearing fruit in patience. Modesty disposes sweetly, patience protects valiantly. One is decorous, the other longsuffering. Wherefore to both are linked 'the choicest of fruits' as the consummation and end of their activities.

7. We should have passed on now to treat of the aromatic trees, the more delicate species, the sprays of henna and nard, if the pomegranates were not still drawing us by their fragrance and delaying our sermon from hastening to other topics. The parable of the pomegranates regards ourselves, for by rule we live together in communities and are united in one Order like seeds beneath one rind. Yes, may we

Jm 3:17

Pr 31:25

Jm 3:17

Jm 3:18

imitate these seeds, resembling them not only by
unanimity in union of heart but also by the embrace,
as it were, of our Order. Practically indistinguishable
in appearance, the seeds of the pomegranate cling
together; they are distinguishable rather by numerical
individuation than by appearance. Let us also learn to
differ from one another in number, not in spirit. Seeds
neither quarrel with one another, not grumble about
the rind, nor try to break through it. They patiently
permit themselves, as it were, to be shut up in its
core, that somehow they may seem to say: 'Behold,
how good and pleasant it is, when brethren dwell in
unity'!*[6] In this Order of ours, brothers, as if in the   *Ps 132:1*
rind of a pomegranate, does not the color of Christ's
passion glow red by our imitation? Yes, like the
seeds of this fruit are they who consider it second
nature to be united under the rind of regular discipline and regard themselves not as constrained but as
protected.[7] Let there be no love of property, no love
of private ownership and then you appear as a seed
of this fruit. Allured by our example, let others
learn 'how good and how pleasant it is to dwell'
in close communion and beneath the defence of a
rind. Let charity unite and the rind defend. However
many communities of an Order you see, regard all as
so many pomegranates which have issued from the
fountain of baptism. Yes, as we read, 'the believers
had one heart and one soul'.* From believers as from   *Ac 4:32*
the seeds of so many congregations living in an
orderly way and in unity of spirit, pomegranates
have developed. Those first communities of believers
were not yet bound by the institute of any Order but
by the impulse of love. To dwell in unity they considered not only useful, not only good but also
pleasant, like the ointment 'which flowed down on   *Ps 132:1-2.*
the beard, the beard of Aaron, to the hem of his   *Lam 15-16,*
robe',* from the Head himself, Christ Jesus, who lives   *nn. 55, 57,*
and reigns for ever and ever. Amen.   *61, 62, 19;*
     n. 80.

NOTES ON SERMON THIRTY-FIVE

1. G. addresses one individual, except in the first two-thirds of par. 1, and in par. 7, where also *te exhibes* occurs. Jean Leclercq has summarized and set in their context Gilbert's three sermons, 35-37, in his article 'The Monastic Tradition of Culture and Studies', *American Benedictine Review,* 11 (1960) 99-131, esp. pp. 116-117. See also Emile Bertaud, 'Hortus, hortulus, Jardin Spirituel', in DSp 7 (1969) 766-784, and for later influence: Stanley Stewart, *The Enclosed Garden: tradition and image in seventeenth-century poetry* (Madison: U. of Wisconsin Press, 1966). Other sermons of Gilbert speak of the garden of wisdom, of the bride, of the Bridegroom, of delights and of heaven; see index.

2. Reading *penetrale* with mss Paris 9605 (apparently), 8546, Madrid 512, Mab. for *penetral* of ms Bruges 49, Troyes 419, or *penetrat* of Migne.

3. Leclercq, 'Otia Monastica,' 92:46.

4. Wisdom is channelled to us both through the fountain and the book; but both, in disclosing Wisdom, leave Wisdom enclosed and hidden. 'Sprays' of the translation is ambiguous; it includes both the sprays of water from the fountain and the sprays or plants which spring up from irrigation. See à Lapide, 8:76.

5. Ps 6:7. *Pro octava* appears in the Vulg. title of Psalms 6 and 11, and in 1 Ch 15:21, *in citharis pro octava canebant epinicion.* Three cantors 'were to clash the cymbals of bronze', eight players 'were to play the keyed harp', and six others 'giving the beat, were to play the *octave lyre'*, 1 Ch 15:20-21 in the translation of The Jerusalem Bible. Thanks to some help from the monks of *Notre Dame des Prairies,* I can say: a) that Psalm 6 *pro octava,* the first of the penitential psalms, was neither appropriate for nor used for a feast or its octaves; b) that Hebrew music did not observe our diatonic scale; c) that commentators suggest either an eight-stringed instrument, *pro octava,* or d) according to the shemînîth, a lower pitch for harps, in contrast with the alamoth or higher pitch for psalteries.

6. See à Lapide, 8:79.

7. Leclercq, 'Disciplina', in DSp 3 (1957) 1291-1302.

SERMON 36
THE SPICES OF ALL THE VIRTUES

*The bride produces spices of all the virtues.
1. In Scripture, the number seven means perfection or spirituality. 2. The meaning of the
mystical trees; labor is sweetened by love or
joy. 3. Action and contemplation blend into
the fruits of the Spirit. 4. The meaning of
henna, nard, and saffron. 5. The Bridegroom
adapts his teaching to the capacity of his
audience. 6. Some trees of our time lack faith
and virtue. 7. The four cardinal virtues: fortitude in cedar, faith which informs prudence in
Lebanon, temperance, self-control and justice
in myrrh, and purity in aloes.*

YOUR SPRAYS ARE A PARADISE OF POME-
GRANATES, WITH THE CHOICEST OF FRUITS,
HENNA WITH NARD, NARD AND SAFFRON,
CALAMUS AND CINNAMON, WITH ALL TREES
OF FRANKINCENSE, MYRRH AND ALOES, WITH
ALL CHIEF SPICES[1]*

Sg 4:13

We must begin with henna, for there we ended. Here are listed seven aromatic trees which are said to sprout from the sealed fountain. Indeed these words seem to be the words of a sealed book.* Yes, the words are sealed and locked. Why do you set before us, good Jesus, the praises of your bride, if you yourself do not disclose what meaning they lock inside?[2] You hold the key of this garden enclosed; you have

See S 35:4

sealed it. Please unseal it! Please unfasten it! Please unfasten, I pray, these seven seals! No one knows what are those intimacies of the bride, those secrets of yours with which her interior is filled. No one knows but you and someone to whom you choose to reveal them.* Would that we too might be the ones who could contemplate with face unveiled the glory of the bride which is from within.* Great is her glory in the mystery both of this number and of these names.

Mt 11:27

2 Co 3:18;
Ps 44:14

Here, as far as by the Lord's gift we can make out, the hidden meaning of the number seven indicates either the spirituality or the universality of graces. Indeed it is a frequent practice of sacred Scripture to use the number seven to designate gifts which are perfect and come from above. There are 'varieties of gifts' and 'varieties of ministries' and 'varieties of services', but 'the same Spirit who apportions to each one as he wills'.* He allots some gifts to some and other gifts to others, but in the bride he collects, as it were, and assembles all together. They are not allotted to her one by one, as if they were divided in her. To others he both apportions and grants; to her he does not so much apportion as grant the whole; unless you understand him to apportion, in as much as he gives her[3] what is choice and privileged, either more graces of the same genus or more in another species. He might have listed other aromatic trees but seven are enough for that meaning we mentioned, either spirituality or universality.

1 Co 12:4-11

2. Now let us discuss the names and natures of these trees. It seems pleasant to linger beneath their shade and their fruit will be sweet to our palate. Their shadow I take to be the symbol, their fruit the reality. How will the fruit of their interpretation not be sweet, when their names sound as pleasant as the rustling of leaves? And you know what a joyful feeling the repetition of such musical words gives to your ear. These words could have been enough to arouse your aesthetic sense. Indeed their simplicity is enough for this sense, yet not enough for the understanding. We must humor the understanding, which longs to

feed on the truth in our sensations. The refrain of
these musical words rings pleasantly in the ear:
'Henna with nard, nard and saffron, calamus and
cinnamon, myrrh and aloes.' Perish the thought that
their meaning is not much more pleasing!

Great are our bodily delights in the trees listed
here, but how much greater are the spiritual delights
which are symbolized by them! 'Your sprays,' says
the Bridegroom, 'are a paradise of pomegranates';
they are also 'henna with nard'. Good indeed is this
sequence: after the labors of patience, after the shyness of modesty, to progress to ointments and royal
ointments. Yes, from the seed of henna also a royal
ointment is wont to be compounded. Now as in
pomegranates we understood the unity of spirit
under a Rule, so in these words and in royal ointments interpret some surpassing sublimity. 'He who
humbles himself,' says the Lord, 'shall be exalted.'* *Lk 14:11.*
In patience and unity of spirit what is meant but *Lam 15, n. 56.*
humility? Humility neither rages against the insolent
nor overreaches its comrades. In pomegranates then
is humility, in henna sublimity; in the former toil, in
the latter delights.

The seed of henna, they say, is wont to be boiled
in oil, that ointment may be pressed from it.[4] Others
sow seeds in tears, but the bride in oil.[5] Our seeds are
our good deeds. If these show cheerfulness they
are, as it were, boiled in oil. To be dipped in oil is not
sufficient; they must be cooked and compounded in
oil and, as it were, changed into the oil itself. What is
boiled in hot oil is steeped in the nature of oil itself.
The seed of henna and the oil are cooked and compounded into an ointment of one consistency. Wonderful indeed is the compound of labor and laughter,
so much more wonderful because in labor not the
labor but the laughter alone is experienced. Indeed
when work is boiled in the oil of exultation work
passes into the essence of the oil. Work itself, so to
speak, forgets it is work, while it is wholly steeped in
the unction of love. But even interior exultation itself
is strengthened and thrives on work; thus indeed the
seed contributes to the oil and the oil to the seed,

when the bride sets out to work with exultation and
thanks to her work, exults the more.

3. This ointment is for royalty. Jesus himself is
gladly anointed with it 'for God loves a cheerful
giver'.* Although 'God the Father anointed him
with spirit and power',* although he was 'anointed
with the oil of gladness more than his fellows',* he
wishes to be anointed by his fellows and longs for the
ointment of our devotion. Who will give me such a
store of oil, that in this oil all the fruits of my works
can be boiled and my heart wholly dissolved? John
the Evangelist, an example of contemplative life and
a symbol of the bride, was lowered into a cauldron
full of boiling oil.[6] Who will give me such abundance
of oil and of boiling oil that I may be wholly immersed and compounded? Who will give me such
abundance of oil and henna seed as may suffice for
the compounding of ointment? This boiling in oil
does not accept every seed, does not welcome every
fruit. Scripturally, not every work can be mingled
with the gladness of contemplation.* Works involv-
ing outward solicitude and the practice of contemplation cannot be compounded together or jell into
one kind of ointment.

What fruits then does this compounding accept?
Those to be sure which the apostle lists: The fruits of
the Spirit are joy, peace, patience, longanimity, faith,
meekness, modesty, self-control, chastity.* These
fruits blend with the oil of contemplation and, as it
were, join together into a natural unity. But especially
suited to this compounding is that seed of which the
Lord speaks: 'The seed is the Word of God.'* In
Scripture also the seed of henna has some resemblance
to manna, which we take as a symbol of the Word of
God. For each of the two, manna and henna seed, is
white and like coriander seed.*

The law of the Lord is spotless.* His law does not
want to be diluted with the water of worldly
wisdom nor to be strengthened by worldly maxims
but by the oil of the Spirit, that its spiritual meaning
and the unction of the Spirit may be pressed from his
law. Meditation on the law and the joy of

Margin references:
2 Co 9:7
Ac 10:38
Ps 44:8

Ps 44:8

Ga 5:22-23

Lk 8:11

Ex 16:31; Nb 11:7.
Ps 18:8

contemplation are most readily blended, when zeal for the word and the oil of grace are joined together in contemplation, and provided the one is boiled in the other, from the process is readily expressed that understanding and unction of the Spirit which 'teaches about all things'.* Notice also that our text does not say simply 'henna' but 'henna with nard'. The Lord admits that he was anointed with nard in preparation for his burial.* What else then do you understand in 'nard' but peace of mind? This nard then is joined with henna, because all practice of contemplation needs peace of mind.

1 Jo 2:27

Mt 26:12. See à Lapide, 8:80.

4. 'Henna with nard, nard and saffron', says the Bridegroom. A good association, for saffron, a flower of a golden color, is related to the golden hue of wisdom. Therefore by henna is meant investigation, by nard vacation and by saffron the vision of wisdom.[7] Nard is rightly placed in the center as a prerequisite for both investigation and vision. For without mental leisure, truth can neither be investigated nor, if it be found, can it be envisioned. Translate henna then as study, nard as leisure and saffron as the fruit of both. In future do not say, O bride, do not say that 'I am swarthy'; call yourself colorless no longer.* For now, on the evidence of the Bridegroom himself, you are resplendent with the color of saffron, because you are radiant in saffron. Rightly is she resplendent with the hue of saffron, for silliness does not make her swarthy, nor does tedium or faintheartedness dye her the color of death, but the golden hue of wisdom and the radiant glow of charity reflects her merriment.

Sg 1:5. See à Lapide, 8:80.

5. Should we wish to refer these plants to the person of Christ, clearly an apt meaning results. Who has been more steeped in the boiling oil of grace? He is recognized in manna; he assumes the appearance of henna seed; pressed on the Cross of his Passion he poured out the mysteries of salvation and the ointments of grace. He suffers in henna, is buried in nard, and in saffron he rises again from the heart of the earth. He is like a fresh and radiant bloom when through his Resurrection his flesh blossomed anew.

And perhaps he ascends into heaven as the calamus.
This tree grows high indeed. His bride shares his suffering, as it were, in henna, is buried with him in
nard, and rises with him in saffron. What follows but
that she should ascend with him in calamus? For if
she has risen with the Bridegroom, she must 'seek
the things which are above', develop her 'taste for
things above', where her Bridegroom is 'enthroned at
Col 3:2   the right hand of God'.*

'Calamus and cinnamon.' Calamus rises high; cinnamon hardly lifts its head from the ground. As the
calamus she looks aloft, but as cinnamon she refrains
Rm 11:20   from lofty thoughts.*[8] The calamus mounts high,
the cinnamon bends low. The bride is the calamus
when she is carried off to God; she is the cinnamon
when she bends down to us. Although she bends
down to us, all she brings forth is spiritual. Indeed
when cinnamon is broken, it emits a visible incense.
But when is it broken, if not when it is opened, when
it is exposed? So indeed when Jesus took bread, he
Mt 14:22.   broke and shared it.* As a teacher accommodating
Lam 172, n. 15.   himself, as it were, he breaks himself when he begins
to open himself, to disembowel himself of the mys-
teries from on high which lie hidden within him, to
eviscerare...eructat.   disgorge from his memory his store of sweetness.*
This is why as broken cinnamon he is said to emit a
visible incense. Why an incense and why visible? An
incense because what he utters is spiritual; visible be-
Jn 11:14.   cause he teaches openly.*
Lam 16, 63.
Now the man who slips from the sublime to the
ridiculous and to empty tales does not bend down
but falls on his face. He does indeed speak in a broken
voice but he does not emit a sweet incense. Like calamus sprouting in water, he rises high amid prayerful
tears. Beautiful is your ascent, but take care that your
descent be like cinnamon. When some reasonable
cause recalls and restrains you from that ascent and
transport, be like cinnamon. Let your chats and your
ordinary behavior have the incense of grace. And if
sometimes you are diverted from your will and
resolve, let your will be bent and, as it were, broken
to the will of an elder; let no murmur be heard, no

complaint. Be cinnamon; emit the incense of grace and not an insulting remark. The reason why broken cinnamon emits a visible incense is that the virtue of humility makes progress and is tested in the weakness of being distressed and, as it were, of being broken. This is called both incense and visible: incense because tranquillity is preserved in your heart; visible because tranquillity reflects on your countenance.

6. To these plants the Bridegroom adds all the trees of Lebanon. Notice too that he lists none but the trees of Lebanon and omits none which belong to Lebanon: 'With all the trees of Lebanon,' he says. Trees of Lebanon are free from rot because they are of cedar and are pure because they are of Lebanon. Only the trees of the Church possess 'the mystery of faith in a pure conscience'* and, as it were, *1 Tm 3:9* immunity from rot thanks to self-control; only the trees of Lebanon possess both purity and permanence. A good tree is obviously a man of the Church in whom strength of discipline and beauty of faith merge and meet. Strength and beauty are his clothing.* *Pr 31:25*

In our day some trees have sprung up which the heavenly Father did not plant, trees not planted in our Lebanon. They make a display of strength in activity, of indifference to insults, of endurance in scarcity. They appear to be of cedar but not the cedar of Lebanon, because their mind and conscience are unclean. Indeed 'to unbelievers nothing is clean'.* *Tt 1:15* The bravery flaunted with a flourish in their behavior becomes rotten in their profession of faith. What glitters, as it were, in their behavior, in their faith offends the nostrils. In their work, of course, piety is apparent; in their questioning, unbelief is patent. Their strength is the strength of a stone and their flesh is of bronze.* To be sure they are true to their *Jb 6:12* father, of whom the Lord speaks in Job: 'His heart is as a stone, unyielding as a blacksmith's anvil.'* *Jb 41:15*

Perversely brave are they, not for the faith but against the faith. Indeed the Almighty has not softened their hearts, has not softened or cleansed or

Rm 14:23

made them white by faith; therefore they are not
trees of Lebanon. 'Whatever does not proceed from
faith is sin';* how much more sinful then is what
attacks the faith! They are not trees of Lebanon
whom purity of faith does not water. Barren are virtues not made fertile through faith, and even faith it-

Jm 2:17, 20

self without virtues is dead.* No rot of incontinence
defiles the purity of faith. In trees of the Church
both meet: the beauty of faith and the strength of
good deeds. Such a cedar is planted in our Lebanon.
Here and not elsewhere exists the purity of faith and,
as it were, a durable and incorrupt perseverance in
virtue.

7. Yes, here 'myrrh and aloes with all chief
spices' flourish. These spices are known to preserve
from corruption even what of itself is liable to corruption. After the cedars of Lebanon why should the
garden grow these spices, if they are indistinguishable from cedar? Although cedars and spices seem
similar, they have their differences. The trees of
Lebanon in themselves possess freedom from corruption, while myrrh and aloes impart incorruptibility to what is corruptible. Cedars are immune
from rot, spices communicate such immunity. He is a
good tree then and rightly planted in the Lord's
paradise, on his noble mountain, on Mount Lebanon,
who restrains himself from disintegrating through
lawlessness and by the myrrh of his message makes
others immune to such disintegration, for his body is
like cedar and from his lips myrrh is distilled.

'Myrrh and aloes with all chief spices.' In our
interpretation, we can refer these spices to the four
cardinal virtues, if in cedar we understand fortitude,
in Lebanon faith which fashions prudence itself, in
myrrh temperance, self-control and justice, and in
aloes purity, for the gum of this tree is said to be a
purgative. By myrrh then outward actions are re-
strained; by aloes inward actions are not feigned
hypocritically. In these now you have expressed the
four cardinal virtues: first constancy, lest you 'believe for a while and in the time of temptation fall

Lk 8:13

away';* then prudence, that your service may be

reasonable;* thus the myrrh of bodily mortification will follow, when you have zeal according to knowledge; in the fourth place aloes, when the heart itself is offered and burnt in sacrifice, so that together there may be in myrrh mortification of the flesh* and in aloes cleansing of the conscience from dead works to serve the living God,* lest we serve to please the eye or to give satisfaction to men instead of to God.* Is not the bride truly blessed, to whom so many terms of endearment are spoken? Much has been entrusted to her, for she manifests so many gifts pleasing to her Beloved.⁹ For in all these he glories and he compliments his bride on her gifts, Jesus Christ who lives and reigns for ever and ever. Amen.

Rm 12:1

2 Co 4:10

Heb 9:14

Col 3:22

NOTES ON SERMON THIRTY-SIX

1.   G. addresses one individual, except in the first sentences of par. 2, *scitis.*

2.   Reading *veritatis* with mss Paris 9605, 8546, Bruges 49, Madrid 512, Troyes 419, rather than *virtutis* preferred by Mab. and Migne.

3.   Reading *illi* with mss and Migne for *ilii* of Mab.

4.   Reading *exprimatur* with mss Paris 9605, 8546, Bruges 49, Madrid 512, Troyes 419, for *exprimitur* of Mab.

5.   Reading a period after *oleo* with mss and Mab. but omitted by Migne.

6.   Jerome, *Adversus Jovinianum,* 1:26, who quotes Tertullian, *De praescriptione,* 36.

7.   Leclercq, 'Otia Monastica,' 120:32.

8.   See à Lapide, 8:81; Jean Leclercq, 'Caelestis Fistula,' in *Verbum et Signum,* Erster Band, Beiträge zur mediävistischen Bedeutungsforschung (Wilhelm Fink Verlag, Munich, 1975) 59-68.

9.   Reading *dilecto* with mss and Mab, for *dilectio* of Migne.

SERMON 37
A WELL AND A FOUNTAIN,
WISDOM AND LOVE

The lover is a well and a fountain, wise and loving. 1. The fountain in the garden is unfailingly fruitful. 2. Irrigating the flower beds of the virtues. 3. The gardens growing in monastic houses distinguish monastic from secular perfection. 4. How wells and fountains differ. 5. How acquired and infused wisdom differ; dispositions needed for wisdom. 6. There are wells of quarrel and accusation, heretical and schismatic. 7. Worldly pleasures are deceptive and fleeting; knowledge of mysteries here is obscure, there is clear. 8. The violence of love; faith and Christ compared to Lebanon. 9. The faithful were once unconquerable against persecution; caution against soft and lukewarm monks.

A FOUNTAIN OF GARDENS, A WELL OF LIVING WATERS, WHICH FLOW IN A TORRENT FROM LEBANON*[1]

Sg 4:15

A fountain of gardens, a well of living waters, which flow in a torrent from Lebanon.' At the beginning of this passage the bride was called a fountain and now at the end her Beloved greets her with the title of fountain. She begins in fruitfulness and her fruitfulness grows with her years;* the ending corresponds with the beginning. Many are the sprays of this fountain but the bride is not exhausted by these sprays. She does not

Ps 91:15

run dry with the passing of time; she is not drained by this overflow. At the beginning of this passage she is called a 'fountain sealed',* and here is a hint that the fountain did not run dry. There is taught the quality of the sprays, here how unfailing they are. Copious streams of graces flow from this fountain and yet the fountain always goes on.[2] This fountain does not withdraw from its origin and so both there and here is called a fountain.

Sg 4:12

But now notice where its waters flow. Where but in gardens? Indeed this is a fountain of gardens and it flows gently because it does not desert the gardens; it is not meant to cleanse but to irrigate; its whole purpose is not to scour filth but to increase fruitfulness. To use a fountain for scouring is good but to use it to increase fertility is better. One washes out stains, the other leaves deposits of graces as if in a delta; one makes plants clean, the other makes them luxuriant. One is open for the scouring of the sinner and of the menstruant woman,* the other is sealed for the delights the other is sealed for the delights of the bride. blemish in you.'* Therefore she is called a fountain only of gardens, a fountain of delights.

Zc 13:1

Sg 4:7

2. From our text, as the measure of heavenly delights is varied and multiple, so the number of gardens seems to be multiplied. One is all red with the rose, another all white with the lily, and a third all purple with violets. There are as many gardens as there are flower beds of virtues. Where one lonely flower blooms, who will claim that a garden is there? So neither one plant of chastity nor one of justice can satisfy the fulness of a garden. Solomon, who was called delicate and gentle,* laid out for himself gardens and orchards and planted them with trees of every kind. He does not say, 'I planted them with a tree' but 'with trees', not 'of one kind' but 'of every kind'. 'I constructed for myself,' he says, 'pools of water to irrigate the forest of budding trees.'* He was indeed rich in delights, for he possessed not a scattering of trees, few enough to be numbered and recorded, but a whole forest, 'a forest of budding trees'. In the garden of wisdom, of course, nothing is

Pr 4:3

Qo 2:5-6

barren, no plant is without buds.

Thus the bride too has many gardens and she is richly planted with saplings of virtue of every kind. In a later chapter also the Bridegroom compliments the bride in the words: 'Since you dwell in my gardens my friends harken to you; make me hear your voice.'* And with every right! For what is it but pleasant to harken to her who dwells in gardens and speaks from gardens? Her voice is not heard in the streets or outside the garden; therefore he is a friend who dwells with her in gardens. He is not so much in gardens as he is the garden himself. She is a garden and he is a fountain watering her gardens with the streams of his teaching. Happy is the bride whose only business is to water the gardens.

Sg 8:13

3. In this crowded gathering,[3] are there not as many gardens as there are spirits? Through unity in spirit there is one garden; through different graces there are many gardens. In these gardens may 'no root of bitterness' raise its head;* may there exist no worthless tree, nothing which ill becomes the garden of the bride. May there be no garden of greens here for 'green herbs will quickly wither'. 'Let him who is weak eat green herbs', says Paul.[4] But you do not need green herbs, as if you were weak. For what is weak in you is stronger than in people of the world. Their weakness finds rest in what is lawful; yours toils towards what is perfect. Their weakness is to rely on what is allowed; yours to stop just short of what is perfect. For you what else is it to be weak, but to be less than perfect? For you what else is it to be weak but not to reach the summit of perfection? And what is it to be strong, but to strive to reach the summit?

Heb 12:15

Therefore our weakness is stronger than weakness in people of the world and, I may say, better is the weakness of a monk than of a person of the world who behaves well.[5] How great would deeds be considered which among us are regarded as weak, if such deeds were seen performed by them? Solid food is for the perfect; yet whoever among us is imperfect disdains a diet of green vegetables. What is lawful for the weak of the world is neither set before us nor demanded by us. What we profess is perfect, even if its execution be weak. What we plant is perfect, though its growth be feeble. Our plants must be watered that they may grow but with waters of the spirit. Paul knew well with what waters to irrigate each garden. To married folk he allows the use of marital intercourse;* the fainthearted he encourages, the weak he helps;* to those still of the flesh he gives milk to drink;* he speaks of wisdom to the spiritual who judge all things, a wisdom however not of this world but from God, wisdom hidden in mystery.*

And if anyone else speaks of the 'beauty of the Lord, the place where his glory dwells',* the delights of the bridal chamber, the joy with which the Bridegroom rejoices over the bride and with which in turn she rejoices in the Lord, obviously he ought not to irrigate a vegetable garden with such waters. Indeed 'the unspiritual man does not receive the gifts of the Spirit of God'.* And in general, does not anyone who either gives spiritual directives for action or sets forth spiritual principles for the understanding seem to you to overflow like an unsullied fountain in aromatic gardens? Truly he is unsullied, for thanks to the perfection of his hearers who harken in gardens, he needs only to discuss the purity of spiritual life and, as it were, to lead the occupants of paradise to drink from the streams of paradise.

4. In this interpretation, take the garden to be the hearers, the fountain the teachers. But if teachers are a fountain, how are they a well? Now you know how different from each other are the fountains and the wells of our experience. A well is dug; a fountain flows of its own accord. In a well waters are stored; from a fountain waters emerge, even presenting themselves unsought. Great is the difference between them, nor can the qualities of one be found in the other interchangeably. A fountain cannot claim the distinctive features of a well or a well those of a fountain; each is confined to the limits of its own nature. On earth our physical sources of water are limited but resources of the spirit bubble over. If

1 Co 7:5-6

1 Th 5:14

1 Co 3:2

1 Co 2:6-7

Ps 25:8

1 Co 2:15, 14

we refer our sources of water to resources of the spirit, it will be possible to find a fountain and a well in the same person and the qualities of each source shared with the other.

Let us then communicate the qualities of each one to the other if you wish and in one person let us point out both qualities. In the fountain let us recognize a sufficiency of doctrine, in the well its hidden nature; in the fountain abundance, in the well deep mysteries. Yes indeed, he is a good teacher who as from a deep well so from a hidden treasure of wisdom 'provides wealth new and old'.* He is a well, *Mt 13:52* because 'the thoughts of God no one comprehends except the Spirit of God'. 'For the Spirit searches everything, even the depths of God',* and like a *1 Co 2:11, 10* fountain he brings everything out into the open to irrigate the gardens of the virtues.* So in the well *Is 58:11* you have hiddenness, in the fountain abundance; profusion in the fountain and profundity of meaning in the well. Here is a deep well which requires no bucket, a fountain which flows freely. 'If anyone thirsts, let him come and drink'* of the waters of the *Jn 7:37* bride, of the waters of Beersheba, that a new Solomon may be born of her fountain. Now Beersheba means the 'seventh well',[6] that is, the well of repose, the well of wisdom. For in the list of spiritual gifts wisdom comes in the seventh place in ascending order.[7]

5. As the well of wisdom is mentioned so also is the fountain of wisdom.* And perhaps in these two *Si 1:5* sources twin channels of wisdom are indicated: one which occurs through investigation, the other through inspiration. The waters of a fountain break out without priming, but in a well the mass of earth is broken through and its solidity penetrated that you may reach living water. Each is necessary to the other, industry to grace and grace to industry, and they offer each other mutual help. For the well-digger toils in vain, if the fountain of life does not flow without priming. But you will have dug yourself a well and prepared a reservoir for water to no purpose, if your well has been abandoned and clogged

with silt; living waters will not descend into it, they 'will not flow in a torrent from Lebanon'.* The waters which cascade from Lebanon can be channeled only into a clean well and waters which flow in a torrent long for a capacious well. You will make the well of your heart deep and capacious if you remove earthly cares, if you prepare a place in your spirit for spiritual joy, if you open your mouth to draw in the spirit and if streams of living water flow into your heart.*

For this work 'your settings were prepared on the day of your birth', as Ezechiel wrote of the King of Tyre.* The capacity for natural intelligence, with which on the day of your creation you were privileged above other living creatures, serves in place of a vast reservoir for receiving and holding the waters of vision and of life. Indeed we read of the well of the Living and All-seeing One.* If after sin, however, your well appears to be obstructed by vices either inborn or acquired, let faith clear it, let hope constantly dig deep into it, let love expand it. Let leisure and freedom from preoccupation not allow it to be blocked with filthy silt. For festive joys demand minds free from anxious cares and the vision of God claims leisure for its exercise.[8] Does he not seem to you to be a deep well, 'in whom are hidden all the treasures of the wisdom and the knowledge of God'?* Will you deny that Mary was like a well of purest water, for she 'stored all the words' which concerned Christ 'pondering them in her heart'?* Do you also be such a well according to your capacity, a well deep and full.

6. Having abandoned the wells of Quarrel and of Accusations, Isaac dug two more: the well of Expanse and the well of Plenty.* In the former he began no longer to contend with vices; in the latter he began to delight in the fruit of virtue. He was unwilling to share a well with the Philistines, whose name means 'Falling in their Drink'. To the Philistines he abandoned the wells of Quarrel and Accusations. They fall prostrate, of course, who drink from the well of error and schism. Their authors dig for their

Sg 4:15

Ps 118:131;
Jn 7:38

Ezk 28:13

Gn 16:14

Col 2:3

Lk 2:19, 51

Gn 26:20-23

adherents to drink from such wells. So did Arius dig, so did Donatus. The one brought Quarrel into the faith, the other broke into factions the bond of brotherhood. Arius, by his heretical definition, introduced degrees into the equality of the Trinity; Donatus, by his presumption, divided into factions the unity of the Church.[9] Dathan and Abiram dug wells of Quarrel against Moses and Aaron, and themselves fell into the pit which they had made, for the earth swallowed them alive.* They fell headlong thanks to the drink for which they themselves had dug, illustrating by the result the name of the Philistines.

Nb 16

But good is the well, when the man who drinks of its water will lift up his head* and not stumble after the drink. He digs a pit for himself, who bores into the solid ground of Scripture with the keenness of his earthly understanding and violently scatters the little garden of the Church, producing some unheard of dogma and obscure mysteries. So does the man who by subtle scrutiny and wily scheming bores into the solid wall of brotherly love and discloses a vein of discord, who encloses and seals himself in the well of plots, not consenting to emerge but sinking deeper and deeper into the cavern of schism and excavating its depth.

Ps 109:7

This is the well of the Philistines; have nothing to do with it. Imperceptibly at first and secretly the waters rise and seep from the pit of an earthy and sensuous mind,* until afterwards they tumble like rapids; but they do not flow from Lebanon. These waters are not reliable;* they are not living waters. Discord cannot remain in harmony; among those who beget schism lasting peace cannot be maintained. Schism is disloyal to itself; it cannot hold together very long because it strives to break up the cement of charity. If anyone should invite you to these wells, wreck if you can the wells of the Philistines and drain dry their pestilential waters; abandon to the Philistines their wells, their wells of Accuasations.

1 Co 15:47;
Jm 3:15

Is 33:16

7. Search for wells of heavenly delights, the wells

of reliable waters and of living waters, which flow in a
'torrent from Lebanon'.* Be a blossom of the garden,
of the garden enclosed, that you may not be plucked,
and you will see how the Lord will open fountains
and torrents for you.* Live your life in the garden
in the hope that you may be changed into a well and
from your bosom 'will flow streams of living water'.*
What are living waters but waters which never fail?*
Good indeed are the waters, a draught of which slakes
without fail the thirst of desire. The allurements of
world without exception exhibit a false appearance
of refreshment and allay worldly concupiscence only
for a moment. As suddenly as they rise, so suddenly
they recede and fail to flow in a continuous channel.
Like a flash flood they suddenly subside and after
the flood it is impossible to find living waters.

Isaac dug in a river bed of a different kind and
found living waters. For there is a flood which seems
sweet but is neither wholesome nor everlasting, like
the worldly flow of pleasure we mentioned above.
Again there is a flood which is wholesome but not
everlasting, and yet if you dig in it you will find
living waters. 'We have confirmation of what was
spoken in prophecies,' says Peter. 'You will do well
to depend on prophecy as on a lamp for lighting a
way through the dark, until the day dawns and the
morning star rises in your hearts.'* This lamp will not
be extinguished in our darkness, for in the meantime
it is needed for our use. But when eternal day dawns,
the lamp of prophetic teaching will end and the flood
of written speech will run dry.[10] Now 'as for prophecies, they will pass away; as for tongues, they will
be silent; as for knowledge, it will disintegrate'.*

By comparison with the revelation to come, the
word of sacred Scripture, so to speak, like a flash
flood flows past with murky water, instructing us as
if 'in a mirror and in riddles'.* But the waters of that
wisdom which is 'face to face'* are true, pure and
everlasting. They will not fail you nor you them.
When the flash flood of our mortality has passed,
with our mortality will pass the mists of mysteries,
and without fog the sparkling waters of the truth

Sg 4:15

Ps 73:15

Jn 7:38
Ps 58:11;
Josh 3:13

2 P 1:19. See Lam,
181, n. 69.

1 Co 13:8

1 Co 13:12

for which we had dug here in our riverbed will merrily well up. Here is the place to look at truth in a mirror, but there to look truth in the eye.[11] Yet to some extent that direct vision of truth invades our foreign soil and, merrily presenting itself to travellers in a place of pilgrimage, invites us to our fatherland. Indeed both the ray of that eternal light and the stream of that eternal river, however festive, are to us still furtive. That ray does not twinkle, that stream does not sparkle, except in gardens, in gardens of perfume. 'O depth of the riches of the wisdom and knowledge of God',* how you resemble a well! You *Rm 11:33* cannot be exhausted; you pour forth living waters, waters wholesome and bountiful.

8. Who will give my little garden these waters and my heart this well of delights? 'From my hidden faults cleanse me, Lord, and from sins not my own spare your servant.'* Make me a Lebanon! 'Sprinkle *Ps 18:13-14* me and I shall be clean; wash me and I shall be brighter than snow.'* 'Cleanse me from the greatest *Ps 50:19* sin and the words of my mouth will be agreeable and the meditation of my heart always in your sight.'* *Ps 18:14-15* Make me a Lebanon, that I may ever pour forth these waters for you. 'They will be agreeable,' says the psalm. What does 'agreeable' mean but that each of two actions will please and will please each of two persons. Who are the two persons but You and I? What are the two actions but my words of praise and my heart's meditation? These are living waters, because they are ever pleasing, ever flowing, but they flow only from Lebanon, and not in a trickle but in a torrent.

A mighty torrent is the experience of passionate love, yet its approaches are gentle, not steep. Mighty is the rush of its torrent, for without let or hindrance it flows right into our affections and gently ebbs away with them. Mighty is its torrents for nothing can check its passion. 'With a torrent from Lebanon'; by naming Lebanon, our text has expressed the reason for its overflow. Purity is the place of overflowing gladness and it pours out waters of saving wisdom; the waters burst from what is bright and make it brighter.

Gather together and, as it were, heap in one pile
these delights. Behold and consider the well, Lebanon, the torrent, the living waters. Herein you will
detect, if you observe in spirit, that these waters are
calm and hidden and powerful and unfailing. The
well denotes hiddenness, Lebanon calmness. In the
torrent all other affection is exhausted; the living
waters cannot be exhausted. A good Lebanon also is
faith, because by faith hearts are purified.* From
this Lebanon of calm understanding living waters
flow; for unless you believe you will not understand.* But good is the understanding when its contemplation remains for ever and ever; this understanding is really alive, for this is eternal life that we
should know the one true God and Jesus Christ
whom He has sent.* And Christ himself is our
Lebanon, pouring living delights in a torrent into
the bosom of his beloved. He is the Lebanon and he is
the stream, since he is the brightness of eternal life
and the purest outpouring. A delightful well assuredly
is the bride's affection, into which the rays of eternal
brightness, like streams from Lebanon, are both
collected and poured out, that they may water the
flowers and gardens of the Bridegroom. Good is the
Lebanon, then, into which nothing defiled makes its
way and mighty is the torrent which cannot be
checked by any obstacle.

9. In Paul's words, the waters flow in a torrent
into the one whom neither persecution, nor hunger,
nor peril, nor nakedness, nor the sword can separate
from the love of Christ.* Among believing peoples,
though so many stumbling blocks of scandal have
been cast in the way and so many monstrous tortures have barred the way, still the waters ever flow
from Lebanon. Indeed the waters are the peoples.*
Great are the obstacles but greater is the torrent. If
you should try to check it, it increases the more and
breaks through the barriers. If dammed up, it rises to
a crest and, gaining momentum from opposition,
overflows more bountifully. For pure love even the
very obstacles towards good,* and virtue under

Ac 15:9

Is 7:9 LXX.

Jn 17:3

Rm 8:35

Rv 17:15

Rm 8:28

provocation increases in value.

If I keep silence, cannot these provocations shake the consciences* of those whose love flows in unpredictable places and times, who love for a season but in the season of trial fall away?* Why do I 'trial'? Even if they suffer not the burden but the mere obstacle of a slight and doubtful temptation, they are easily checked and abandoning their resolution rush back to the world with a force nothing can halt. If you cry after them in the words of the prophet: 'Stay, stay',* not one of them returns. No persuasion calls them back,* not the devoted pursuit of a teacher, not the unhappiness which often and almost always turns up along their ways.* They scatter and rush and stumble, to drink by the wayside from the torrent of pleasure, which will not raise but shatter their heads upon the earth.* 'Blessed indeed are the spotless on their way, who walk in the law' of charity,* who walk in the torrent, wherever the torrent of the Spirit leads.* They do not retreat or become separated by any obstacle from the love of God,* which is in Christ Jesus our Lord, who lives and reigns for ever and ever. Amen.

1 Co 8:12

Sir 37:4; Mk 4:17

Na 2:8
Ga 5:8

Ps 13:3; Rm 3:16

Ps 109:6-7

Ps 118:1
Ezk 1:12

Rm 8:33, 39

NOTES TO SERMON THIRTY-SEVEN

1.   G. writes to one individual, except in par. 4, *nostis . . . vultis . . . habetis.*

2.   *Copiosi ex hoc fonte rivuli gratiarum emanant, et semper tamen fons manet.* The Latin word-play *emanant . . . manet* is frequent.

3.   *Frequenti conventu.* See Lam 15, n. 58; 19, nn. 82, 83.

4.   Paul and Gilbert here lack neither good sense nor good humor. As the Jerusalem Bible comments on Rm 14:2: 'Christians not sufficiently instructed in the faith and therefore without the firm convictions that would give them a sure conscience, vv. 2, 5, 22, considered themselves bound to observe certain days, v. 5, and to abstain from meat or from wine, vv. 2, 21, perhaps as a permanent obligation, v. 21. Such ascetical practices were familiar to the pagan world (the Pythagoreans) and the Jewish (the Essenes, John the Baptist). Paul lays down the same general rule as in the similar case of 1 Co 8; 10:14-13: each must "act for the Lord" as his conscience tells him, vv. 5-6, provided it is not a doubtful conscience, v. 23; but above all, charity must govern the conduct of those "strong" in the faith, vv. 1, 15, 19-21 and 15:1-13.' The early Cistercians would have especially appreciated G.'s good humor, for they were strict vegetarians, abstaining from meat, fowl, eggs and fish at all times, and from milk products including cheese and butter during long months of the year. The monks of *Notre Dame des Prairies* point out that though *olus* does not appear in RB, the pertinent passage, RB 39:1-5, is neatly summed up in the third stanza of the hymn for All Saints of the Order, *Avete Solitudinis:*

> *Vobis olus cibaria / Fuere vel legumina!*
> *Your daily food was beans / Or vegetable greens.*

5.   See Lam 41, with allusion to Si 42:14, and comparison with Bernard SC 12:9, I 66:6-21, and QH 4:3 and 7:14, PL 183: 184A and 184D.

6.   Gn 21:30-31; Leclercq, 'Otia Monastica', 120:29.

7.   Is 11:1-9; Rm 12:8; reading *sapientia* with Mss and Mab. for *sapientiae* of Migne.

8.   Leclercq, 'Otia Monastica', 91:35.

9.   See *Church History,* by Karl Bihlmeyer, rev. Hermann Tüchle, tr. Victor E. Mills (Westminster, Md.: Newman, 1958) on Arius, I, pp. 246-56, on Donatus, I, pp. 264-7. See C.H. Talbot, "Sermones Inediti B. Aelredi Abbatis Rievallensis", Rome: 1952, Intro. pp. 20-23.

10.   *literarius sermo,* an apt title for the literary genre of G.

11.   See J. Chatillon, 'Hic, ibi, interim', RAM 25 (1949) 194-99.

SERMON 38
WINTRY NORTH AND WARM SOUTH WINDS

Within and without, the lover is affected by north and south winds. 1. Gilbert laments the disasters of his day. 2. Scarcity within and oppression without crush the monks but even more their abbot. 3. The ebb and flow of temptation and consolation existed even among the apostles. 4. Persecution, as in the early Church, can be salutary. 5. The north wind within us is tedium and sadness. 6. This is harmless if we are not responsible. 7. Pray to the Lord for those so afflicted.

BEGONE, O NORTH WIND, AND COME, O SOUTH WIND, BLOW THROUGH MY GARDEN, AND LET ITS PERFUMES FILL THE AIR*[1]   *Sg 4:16*

Sweet and holy affections are the perfumes of the bride. For she is his garden. When the south wind blows, her perfumes are diffused for the delights of the Bridegroom but in turn the inclemency of the north wind stops their flow. Chilling is the north wind and when it blows, her perfumes are frozen. How long, O Lord, will the north wind of adversity oppress our regions? How long will it brood over our little gardens? How long, good Jesus, will the frost of the north wind congeal our perfumes? Spare, O Lord, spare your bride from the north wind. Long has its raw and violent blast been driving and oppressing and brooding. From all sides mounting adversity overwhelms us. Command

457

the wind, Lord, to rise and be gone, to allow us to
catch our breath.

The impoverishment of misfortune is barren or
everywhere begets serious disasters. Slender resources
are easily harmed and one abyss of misfortune calls
to another with the roar of your cataracts.* Do you
secretly mount attacks against us,* as if you were saying to the north wind: attack, oppress, plunder?
'Smoke will come from the north,' says Isaiah.* But
not smoke so much as a flame threatens us now, the
flame of a cauldron aboil from the blast of the north
wind.* From the north comes frost and from the
north comes flame. So it is, O Lord, 'In the harshness
of your hand you oppose me';* you check the
streams of your mercy. Therefore my spirit burns and
in my meditation fire will break out.* Burdensome is
this fire of fretful worry and in its heart perfumes
do not spread but rather, if you allow any perfumes
to spread, their flow is dried up, especially when an
opening for misfortunes seems more and more to con-
front us.

2. *Lord, my sorrow is in your sight and 'my
lament is not hidden from you'.* Known to you is
the reason for my anxiety.* I should rather have said
for my grief, for all my anxiety now has begun to
pass into grief. Where no ray of good counsel breaks
through, where even a shadow of fair hope does not
appear, there one plays the role not of anxiety but of
grief. My groans multiply and my heart grieves. Little
ones beg for bread and there is no one to break it for
them,* for there is none to be broken. I do not mean
the bread of the word but this daily food for the
body. Yet my soul cannot be filled with the richness
of that heavenly bread as long as lack of this daily
bread brings on, as it were, the emaciation of grief.
Distracted by the sound of their sobbing, I have forgotten to eat that heavenly bread.

A harsh north wind is exterior hardship, but much
harsher is anxiety of mind. One of the two over-
burdens you, brethren; both together oppress me.
I carry a burden among you because of our common
distress and a distress of my own beyond yours,

Ps 41:8
Jr 9:7-9

Is 14:31

Jr 1:13

Jb 30:21

Jr 20:9

Ps 37:18, 10

Lm 4:4, Lam
175, n. 28

because it is on your behalf. Hence arise cases of
misfortune, hence legal quarrels. Some whisper,
others taunt, and what is beyond human effort to
prevent from happening, they turn into a reproach
when it happens. Some provoke, others mock, attributing bad luck to folly. Good results in which they
rejoice, they ascribe to themselves and consider the
fruit of their foresight or merit, not of God's
bounty. 'The tents of brigands thrive,' says Job, 'and
brashly they challenge God, although he has placed
everything in their hands.'* Some are both brigands   Jb 12:6
and braggarts, for what belongs to God they filch for
themselves in assigning it to themselves; they attribute the gift of God's grace to the effectiveness of
their own effort.² Why do you reproach us with
the blessings dispensed to you from on high? Because
the eye of divine clemency looks kindly upon you,
must your eye look askance at us? Why do God's
blessings make you more ready to depreciate than to
appreciate?

3. *You see, O Lord, on how many sides blasts*
from the north wind assail us. From all sides
troubles, murmuring, reproaches blow upon us. Dis-
tracted and hampered amid such sorrows, the spirit
cannot welcome the gentle breezes of the south
wind. Arise, O Lord; let not the north wind prevail;
long enough now has it been rioting and swooping
upon us; command it to rise and be gone and yield to
the south wind. The cauldron has been boiling now
for a long while before the face of the north wind,*   Jr 1:13
but do you dispatch the south wind, O Lord, to
make the center of this forge like a breeze fresh as
dew. I dare not ask for uninterrupted breezes from
the south; it is enough if the inclemency of the north
wind be moderated even by some alternation with the
south. You stretch the north wind over the void, as
we read in Job,* not over your garden.   Jb 26:7

The little garden of the bride is not empty, for in
it have been planted all the perfumed species listed
above. And how will the glad perfumes of meditation
be able to flow where our studies are not free from
grief, where hardship saddens and the north wind

Ex 20:5

binds? Be a zealot, Lord,* be jealous over the bride, command the north wind to abate and with the south wind to share equal seasons. This will happen, if to match the great number of sorrows in my heart, your consolations bring joy to my soul. You see, brethren, how the north wind might give birth to the south in its own measure and perhaps where the north wind has abounded, the south wind will abound even more. For the south wind will both blow favorably and compensate for the damage the north wind has inflicted. Therefore let the north wind arise, let it rage and bluster to its heart's content, provided it offers an entrance and an opening³ to the breezes of the south.

Do they not seem to you to have endured the bluster of the north wind, whom Paul addresses in the Epistle to the Hebrews: 'You endured a hard struggle with sufferings,' he says, 'sometimes being publicly exposed to abuse and affliction, and sometimes being partners with those so treated. For you had compassion on the prisoners.'* But amid such blasts of the north wind did not the south wind claim its turn? Indeed it did. In Paul, hear what follows: 'And you joyfully accepted the plundering of your property, since you knew that you yourselves had a better possession and an abiding one.'* Again when the apostles 'left the presence of the Council, rejoicing because they had been found worthy to suffer outrage for the name' of Jesus,* does not the south wind seem to you to have breathed gently upon them after the driving attacks of the north?

Heb 10:32-34

Heb 10:34

Ac 5:4

Consider that sad Sabbath when the Lord lay in the tomb. Did the hearts of the apostles not shiver in disbelief and timidity, as if before the blast of the north wind? At the Resurrection of the Lord, a gentle south wind began to blow through his garden. As Scripture shows, throughout these forty days, from many proofs of his Resurrection, both belief in his truth and confidence in his liberation gradually increased. On the very day of Pentecost, when there came a mighty wind into the upper room 'where the apostles were sitting',* all the chill of their minds

Ac 2:2

thawed 'like an inundation in the south',* and
henceforth the fragrance of their word and their
virtues filled the air.

    4. But for all that, did the harsh north wind keep
its peace? Did not the storm of the persecutors and
the blast of heretical tempests arise much more
violently? Did not the north wind of temptation in
jealous rivalry fall upon the south wind of grace?
Like a lone survivor, the north wind attempts to
blow through the garden with the chill of its harsh
blast, trying to prevent perfumes from filling the
air. But so much the further is the perfume carried.
Now stimulated, now lulled in alternate waves of
adversity and prosperity, the bride of Christ, his
Church, did not then and does not now cease to diffuse the perfume of virtues. In persecution her
courage shone bright; in peace her numbers increased.
In persecution the valiant are tested, in peace the
weak are strengthened.

    Yet why do I now recall the primitive Church,
when the Bridegroom's garden still encounters frequent though not so violent assaults of the north
wind? The sound and the north winds take turns
in the garden. In our time a great tempest is driving
the Church and indeed from the north.[9] For from
there the schism originates, from there it rises and
there it lingers; from there like a lone survivor the
north wind is her oppressor. Command it, Lord, to
rise and be gone. Summon the south wind and say:
'Come, blow through my garden, let its perfumes fill
the air.' I do not mean the south wind of earthly
happiness and security, for this south wind often
checks and dries up the perfumes; but summon the
south wind of your grace. And if need be, send the
north wind also into that barren garden, the north
wind not of stubbornness but of trial, that trial
itself may grant understanding to obey when we hear
your command.* Lash your garden with the chill
north wind; as if with blows, rouse it from sloth, that
it may turn more eagerly to the gentle gusts of the
south wind. Not only in different seasons but also in
different regions, the south and north winds blow by

Ps 125:4

Is 28:19

turns in her garden. Just as now the south wind blows
and then the north, so here the south blows and there
the north. Sometimes however both blow together,
but the one outside and the other inside, the north
wind outside and the south inside, the former raging,
the latter assuaging. Let the north wind bluster and
riot outside; only let it not blow through the garden
inside, let it not penetrate within, let it not choke
the interior gladness of the heart which is in Christ.

*When, O Lord, will that freezing wind subside
altogether? When will come the time with no further
fear of its frosty face? Your city has been founded,
your garden planted on the northern slopes. This
wind in Scripture is said to be on the right. That is
why Job utters such a complaint about it: 'At the
right hand of the East my troubles rose up at*

Jb 30:12

once.'[5] *Justifiably he called that wind 'on his
right', since it could not bring him anything sinister!*[6] *Rather it brought the righteous man an
increase of glory, when his courage, once tested,
shone bright and, once challenged, was increased.
From close by, this wind swoops into your garden,
for your garden lies on the northern slopes. Make
this wind favorable to us, O Lord; moderate it with
the breezes of the south wind. For even the north
wind cooperates with us for the blessing of your love,
when the south wind also blows. Whether it arises at
your bidding or by your permission, let not the north
wind of trial make us afraid. For in a little while the
south wind of consolation will follow on its heels,
even if in the meantime the south wind does not
intervene. Indeed where affliction abounded, grace*

Rm 5:23

*also abounded.**

5. But why do I talk to you, brethren, about
outward trial? A different north wind is wont to
molest you. God spares you this outward north wind,
interposing other men to bear the brunt of the frequent assaults of worldly turmoil and trial. No
burdensome outward anxiety ties you in knots,
because by right none touches you; yet anxiety does

Lam 20, n. 85

not leave you immune.* Those whom outward
anxiety cannot affect, inner anxiety afflicts with

boredom. Things go well with them in one region because they are not exposed to outward activities. But none the less they do not escape the north wind, when they are not satisfied with themselves in interior activities. Joys once festive turn to disdain and sadness transforms the cheerful face of the mind.

Happy the man who does not experience this transformation. But who is he? Who is the man whom boredom does not weary at times and sadness exasperate? According to Acts, where we were making headway with fair sailing, there shortly afterwards we run into shallows and over those sailing with a fair wind an opposing gale breaks.* Even when no reason *Ac 27:13-26* is apparent, trouble intrudes. Since its source is not evident, it poses a threat. A man is angry at the anger he suffers without reason, and he loathes the emotion without knowing its source. This harsh spirit breathes where it wills and you know not whence it comes and perhaps where it goes or rather where it ends.[7] For of itself such an emotion goes towards evil, but often it results in good. It does not reach the goal to which it tends but 'God provides a way out even of trial'.* When he wishes he introduces the *1 Co 10:13* north wind; when he wishes he commands: 'North wind, begone!'

If in the meantime you complain of its annoyance, know that thanks to such teaching you are given a reminder and a warning. You are reminded to be aware of the nearness of the north wind, warned to avoid its chill. It is not in your power to escape its neighborhood as long as you dwell on the northern slopes, but you can escape its violence. While we are here, the north wind is always our neighbor. It is not always violent, but after we have wheeled through the north, we often tack back by the south.* Even when you do not feel its assault, be *Qo 1:6* on guard against its proximity.

6. Yet when will you escape its whirlwind, unless the gentle south wind comes when called, and so you may spread your wings to the south wind and grow feathers for the flight to heaven?* If however the *Jb 39:36* north wind strives to intervene and with freezing

blast to check the new growth of your wings, it does
hamper your wings from flight and your perfume
from filling the air. It hampers, I admit, but does not
blow your wings away. Yes, utter boredom and bitterness of heart exercises the virtues without destroying
them. This whirlwind attacks your holy resolve without blowing it away. It checks your happiness; it does
not blow your constancy away.

The spirit is affected by boredom but is not overwhelmed. The spirit is saddened but wrestles with its
sadness. Virtue thus troubled is not less brave but
less happy. What has the spirit in common with
the vice with which it brawls, against which it
declares war? The spirit is not responsible for the
disgust it feels, since it never came to terms with
disgust. The spirit suffers assault but does not sur-
render. According to our text, the spirit itself does
not initiate this struggle but rather the north wind,
on whose slopes it dwells. So the spirit loathes this
disgust, feeling its batteries aimed at virtue.

The spirit attacked by boredom knows with what
boredom it endures being bored with the good life,
how it disdains the disdain, with what bitterness it
wrestles against bitterness, against that violent bitterness which intrudes uninvited into the unchanging
round of regular discipline. The spirit by choice veers
towards the south wind and behold! the north wind
relentlessly interferes, despite the vigorous opposition of the spirit. It is hard to hold out against that
frosty face and it is not in our power to break its
hold. The spirit is worn out both by its boredom with
discipline and by loathing for this boredom. Both
feelings are repugnant: to have no taste for what you
have chosen and to experience what you loathe. Each
is a trial: to protect discipline and to put lethargy to
rout.[8]

7. *How do you tolerate for so long, good Jesus,
so much harassment of your beloved bride? Unwillingly she suffers lethargy and pursues it to punish it
in herself as if it were deliberate. She scarcely endures her inability to delight at will in you who are
her only good. She blames herself for what she*

*suffers unwillingly. One comes from the north wind
to goad her, but his goad spurs the bride to prayer.
Chafed by this goad she casts herself on her knees,
though previously she had made ready for your
embraces.*[9] *Protect your bride, good Jesus, from these
evil days. For unless you help her, her soul will dwell
in the north wind. Who will rise against the north
wind but you, O God, who come from the south? A
good perfume is holy resolution and a pure conscience, but it does not surround a spirit which fails
to enjoy the delights of your blessing. Come, good
Jesus, come; blow through your garden that its perfumes may flow 'like an overflow in the south'.** Ps 125:4
*Your bride is the garden; do you be the south wind.
When you water it, her soul will be like a well
watered garden** and when you blow, her perfumes* Jr 21:12
*will not fail, for you live and reign for ever and ever.
Amen.*

NOTES ON SERMON THIRTY-EIGHT

1.   G. writes to one individual, but note *fratres* in par. 2, *Videtis, fratres,* in par. 3, *vobis, fratres . . . vos,* in par. 5.

2.   Reading *effectum* with mss and Migne for *affectum* of Mab.

3.   Reading *materiam* with mss rather than *quasi vim* preferred by Mab. and Migne.

4.   Sermon 41 was delivered shortly after the death of Aelred of Rievaulx, 11 January 1167, so that one may suppose that Sermon 38 was composed not long before that date. The north wind and the schism here may thinly disguise the quarrel between Henry II and Thomas à Becket. The quarrel hardened with Becket's successful resistance to Henry's attempt to make 'an illegal appropriation of money,' in July 1163 (Mann, X:161). 'This is . . . the first case of any opposition to the King's will in the matter of taxation which is recorded in our national history.' (Stubbs, *Constitutional History of England,* I:463, quoted in Mann.) After what became known as the Constitution of Clarendon (January 1164) and the Council of Northampton (October 1164) Becket escaped to the continent, and from November, 1164 was living at the great Cistercian Abbey of Pontigny. See L. A. Desmond, 'Becket and the Cistercians,' *Canadian Catholic Historical Association* 35 (1968) 9-29.

5.   See de Lubac, *Exégèse,* 2:411.

6.   G. plays on the word 'sinister', which also means 'left'.

7.   *An magis quo evadat?* This is the second half of a double indirect question. Lam 197, n. 179.

8.   Lam 170, nn. 3, 4; 197, n. 180.

9.   Lam 188, n. 120, referring not to S 33:7, but to S 38:7.

SERMON 39
FREEDOM, AFFECTIVITY, AND GRACE

The lover distinguishes freedom, affectivity and grace: 1. Fear is opposed to a good resolution. 2. The spirit of slavery differs from the spirit of freedom. 3. Freedom of choice contributes nothing, if grace is absent; Gilbert discusses freedom of choice. 4. Freedom is not withdrawn in the state of fallen nature; Gilbert distinguishes freedom of our state, of disposition, of affection. 5. Freedom to will the good freely is distinguished from freedom to will the good affectively. 6. All things flow gently and fruitfully from charity and knowledge.

BEGONE, O NORTH WIND, AND COME, O SOUTH WIND, BLOW THROUGH MY GARDEN AND LET ITS PERFUMES FILL THE AIR*[1]

Sg 4:16

E xecute your command, good Jesus; dispatch the south wind from heaven and conduct it into your garden, into the soul of your bride. *By this gentle breeze dispel boredom, dispel sadness from her feelings. For each is a misery and each resembles the north wind; each fetters the mind, as it were, bars access to the current of pure joy. What is the effect of fear? With its chilling harshness does fear not also constrain the affection? Spare your bride, Lord, from feelings not her own. What is more alien to her than a fear which does not exist in charity, since the bride's whole existence is in charity? Fear is enslaving; she has been*

467

called to freedom.

You saw, brethren, in yesterday's sermon,[2] a man proceed fearfully in order to undergo the first elements of formation. With what a slow and stumbling resolve he allowed himself to become initiated into the rudiments of discipline! You know well what generous streams of alms his hands poured out, while he was still a man of the world. What made him hesitate but the north wind of fear in our region, which paralyzed his mind? The south wind, of course, had blown upon part of his mind but did not blow through it; therefore he was quick to scatter abroad the fragrance of almsgiving, but after many efforts at long last scarcely a trickle of that most precious and fragrant perfume of renunciation could be squeezed from his spirit. Obviously he resembled the young man in the Gospel who, having boasted to the Lord of his observances of the Law, when the narrow way of evangelical perfection was set before

Mt 19:16, 22   him, went away sad;* with this difference: the man in Matthew went away sad while our man, although sad, came forward none the less.

Notice the north wind of fear blowing under the Law; therefore few of the precious and choice perfumes filled the air under the Law. But on the day of Pentecost, when the Spirit blew mightily from the south, so many thousands of men poured forward in

Ac 2   the truth, in the word and in the life of the Spirit.* Care for their private affairs did not shackle them for the future.

2. Hearts free from this truly harsh north wind pour themselves out more generously in contemplation and in love of God. 'You did not receive,' says Paul, 'the spirit of slavery to fall back into fear, but you received the spirit of sonship in which we cry:

Rm 8:15   "Abba, Father".'* The former was the spirit of the north wind, the latter of the south; the north grievous, the south gracious. Therefore the bride bids the north wind 'begone', because it is grievous and burdensome and oppressive, but the south wind, joyful and agreeable, is invited to come and blow through the little garden of the Bridegroom.

The north wind brings torture, the south brings rippling laughter. The north is a menace, the south brings waves of caresses and delights. 'I will ask my Father,' says the Lord, 'and he will give you another Paraclete';* this is to invite the south wind and bid it come blow through his garden. 'Blow through my garden and let its perfumes fill the air.'

Jn 14:16

Some fruits do not pour out their juices unless they are squeezed and crushed. But fruits which exist in a garden so delicately described do not wait to be squeezed; they cannot be crushed, but when the south wind blows they pour out their juices gratuitously. Look at the wisdom of the world. Does it not seem to be violently squeezed out and developed by long practice and study? But in the authors of our philosophy the depths of wisdom surge up both speedily and powerfully. Would you hear of its speed? 'When you stand before kings and governors do not think beforehand; it will be given you in that hour, what you should speak.'* Would you hear of its power? 'I will give you a mouth and wisdom which none of your adversaries will be able to withstand.'* How would these words flow so suddenly and so calmly, if the south wind did not blow? You have heard now whence come the perfumes of truth, so plentiful and so apt for the occasion.

Mt 10:18-19;
Mk 9:11

Lk 21:15

3. Has not charity likewise 'been poured into our hearts by the Holy Spirit who has been given to us'?* Many are the perfumes which are poured through the Spirit and only through the Spirit: joy, peace, patience, longsuffering, goodness, kindness, loyalty, meekness, modesty, self-control, chastity.*[3] These have not only come forth but have also poured forth. That they pour forth signifies their abundance; that they pour forth at the breath of the south wind signifies the absence of compulsion. Charity cannot be forced; it flows freely. It is borne along not of necessity but by choice, provided the south wind blows.

Lk 21:14-15

Ga 5:22-23

For what could the liberty of choice contribute, if the south wind of grace did not blow? Wherever choice.exists, choice is always free. But we do not

admit that choice is free to choose all things. Choice
does not have the liberty to choose or to execute all
things. Liberty always exists in making a choice, but
it is not always possible to make a choice. Indeed the
will can only choose freely, but things do exist which
the will cannot choose on its own. The will is its own
master, it is free when it is present; but if the will is
absent, then the spirit is not free for any act which
requires the presence of the will. Nor is the spirit
any more its own master because it controls the will
it has, or because it has a good will. However, in as
far as after the fall the will consists in freedom of
choice, the spirit always wills freely what it wills, but
the spirit has not been left free to will anything it
wishes or even the things it should will.

One freedom exists indeed which does not exist
without the will and without which no will exists;
but another freedom exists which the will does not
always accompany. The former freedom exists in the
will, the latter is in some faculty of willing. The
former freedom exists in the will, the latter, as it
were, is related to the will. The former freedom is in
our power but the latter we coerce. So vision is some
power of seeing in the eye and at the same time
vision is some change which occurs in seeing. So also
in the spirit, understanding is called both a natural
power to understand and the use of that power.

In choice likewise this distinction occurs; in the
same word is expressed both the aptitude and the act.
Freedom of choice exists in both, not only in the
power to choose but also in the act of choosing;
and when the will is exercised in choosing evil, it is
always enslaved. The will indeed is enslaved by the
very fact that it is weak both for good and against
evil. An evil will is free by the very fact that it is
a will but enslaved by the very fact that it is evil. For
Jn 8:34   'everyone who commits sin is the slave of sin'.* Sin
ties in knots and binds the one it seizes; sin makes
him a captive as long as it coerces him.

Ps 125:4   4. *But do you, O Lord, 'change our captivity,
like a flash flood in the south'.* Send forth your
spirit and our primeval freedom will be renewed; it*

will be renewed I say, not created anew. For even if liberty has been obscured, it has not been withdrawn. Liberty remains what it was created to be, but it cannot move itself to what it was created for; it is alive but it does not thrive. So also in madmen their inborn rationality is not lessened but in those so afflicted no movement of reason can thrive. When their great illness has been cured, then reason which was dormant is not given back but is reawakened. So also the liberty of choice congenital to man is neither wholly nor partially withdrawn but is bound fast by sin. It is the same liberty which it was created to be but it has been affected in a different way.

There exist, so to speak, a freedom of our state, a freedom of disposition, and a freedom of affection. The first belongs to our nature and therefore is always good; but unless the first be healed, the second will not aim at goodness or the third exist in goodness. The first consists in a natural aptitude; the second in the habit of a mind which is well or badly constituted; the third consists in actual exercise. Therefore, unless the natural aptitude be assisted by grace, neither the habit of the will nor its actual exercise will look toward virtue. The liberty of choice is weak; so where choice wilts, the south wind will blow and at once perfumes will fill the air. Choice does not have this noble and truly free liberty which exists for goodness and in goodness, unless the Spirit has set it free. *Therefore, O Lord, send forth your Spirit, to bestow through grace both the power to perform and the act of willing, for the Spirit first bestowed the possibility of both when he fashioned human nature.*

We listed three freedoms above: in the third an act of will is present; in the second it is implied; in the first is considered the natural potency directed towards the other two. Therefore let the first be called capacity, the second power, and the third the will. It does not seem to be the same thing to have a natural capacity for something and to have power to perform it. Many things for which we have the capacity by nature, we cannot do at once, when the innate faculty is either hampered by weakness or

lacks skills and exercise. Often the eye cannot see for
the moment; although vision has not lost its natural
capacity; the habit is present but its exercise is absent.
By nature the eye is capable of seeing but in fact the
eye çannot see. Similarly our natural freedom of
choice indeed remains but is hampered by sin, and
therefore is unable to have the third freedom which
is in goodness, or the second which is toward goodness. The first remains, changed indeed but not
diminished; the others must be said not even to
remain. For after sin, to will the good is not left free
to us, so that our freedom, which consists in a good
will, does not remain, but by grace the third freedom is breathed into us, the second is repaired, and
the first is created according to nature.

5. Let this much be said of the freedom by which
we will the good: that it is from grace. But another
freedom exists none the less through grace, by which
we not only will rightly but also will goodness itself
affectively. The former freedom always exists in the
will but the latter does not. Indeed we always will
freely but not always affectively. Feelings have
nothing to do with our liberty of choice. Yet the
freedom of a good will is not wholly free, if it is
without affection. But when the south wind blows, at
once the perfume of affections fills the air. No pressure is exerted to elicit them; they flow freely.
Frequently some boredom and sadness accompany a
holy will; but sweet affections do not share the
journey with boredom and sadness.*

Lam 197, 178

Affections are a perfume to the sense of smell and
equally pleasing to the touch; they are pleasant to
experience and pleasant to remember; pleasantly
they fill the air and pleasantly they are wafted afar.
They fill the air for themselves; they are wafted afar
for others. Both are perfumed, affections within and
aspirations without. The liberty of choice can aspire
to these, but they do not depend on the liberty of
choice. As evil feelings often exist despite a good will,
so good affections when they are present, even if
they exist with a good will, do not flow from it;
good will remains free without them and from them,

as it were, breathes freely. Affections make the will itself more free but affections do not flow from freedom of the will. They flow, however, when the south wind blows through.

O gentle south wind, truly desirable, by whose breath the horrid face of winter frost dissolves and the springtime of jocund freshness smiles in gardens, yes, and a new summer and autumnal fruitfulness! Yes, for in the diffusion of perfumes is meant the ripening of harvests. See how good and how pleasant it is to wait in chambers and in gardens for this breath of perfume so fragrant, renewing and recreating the fruits of the Spirit, pouring out its aroma, scattering its bouquets. *Send this Spirit to us, O Lord, to clothe our little garden with a new countenance after the horror of the north wind, and to change our grief into joy.**

Est 13:17.
Lam 18, n. 78.

Or if the north wind means something good, invite it together with the south wind. Let them combine their functions and let each play its part. Let the north wind bind and the south wind loose; let the north tie wantonness in knots and let the south relax the spirit in rippling laughter. Let the north bestow continence and the south make conscience merry. Let the north restrain and the south replenish. 'I have become like a wineskin in the frost,' says the psalmist, 'yet I have not forgotten your statutes.'* Good is the wineskin thus frozen and filled: outside the frost of continence, inside the fulness of righteousness. Well does each wind blow when our exteriors are stiffened as if by the cool wind of continence and our interiors are thawed with overflowing happiness.

Ps 118:83

6. In order that you may divert the breeze of the south wind to your interior, the bride says 'blow through'. A breeze which blows through, blows into the interior and to it nothing is impenetrable. This breeze is delicate, keen and swift, blowing through without inflating. Knowledge puffs up;* charity blows through. Charity is more intimate than knowledge and reaches to more hidden recesses. The Spirit blows through all that is more hidden, for he searches

1 Co 8:1

1 Co 2:10

even the depths of God.* Where he blows through the depths, there the perfumes of knowledge flow for our use: meditations, prayers, sighs, sobs, tears, and colloquies. All fill the air like perfumes for they originate from charity. All things which proceed from charity are fragrant, full of grace. They are precious and abundant, fragrant and filling the air. They overflow because they proceed from the fulness of charity. They overflow and are not squeezed out nor do they suffer the violence of the wine-press. You read of no wine-press built in this garden, for the south wind fulfills the function of the wine-press. What is breathed upon fills the air better than what is trodden upon. For these perfumes, as we said, are gratuitous, not squeezed out through fear but wafted upon the wind.

Some commentators apply the north and the south winds to the adversity and prosperity of this world.[4] And indeed the Church of God, harassed by this twofold temptation, always abounds in the perfumes of good affections and of a good reputation. Hence she endures the necessity of being sifted by these temptations, because she knows how to survive success and how to suffer want. This passage cries for fuller treatment, but in conclusion let it suffice to have touched the topic but lightly. The next sermon will pass on to the mutual invitations of the bride and the Bridegroom, if Jesus Christ who lives and reigns our God, deigns to grant us his grace.

NOTES TO SERMON THIRTY-NINE

1.   Gilbert uses plurals of address in par. 1 and 2, the singular in par. 6. See Etienne Gilson, *The Spirit of Mediaeval Philosophy,* (N.Y.: Scribners, 1936) 304-323; D. Odon Lottin, *Psychologie et Morale aux XIIe et XIIIe Siècles,* (Louvain: Abbaye de Mont César, 1942) 1:12-20. In his unpublished dissertation, Lam points out that Gilbert uses the word *arbitrium* but avoids *liberum arbitrium* for liberty is included in the word *arbitrium*; Lam suggests a schema for 'liberty' and its three species, of which the following is an adaptation.

	Libertas		
	1) *conditionis*	2) *dispositionis*	3) *affectus*
relata	libertas naturae (libertas arbitrii)	libertas arbitrii & gratia	libertas arbitrii & gratia & affectus
ad Deum	naturaliter creatur	per gratiam reparatur	per gratiam inspiratur
ad nos	in naturali aptitudine	in habitu bene vel male constitutae mentis	in usu
	potentia	potestas	voluntas
ad bonum	invalida	ad bonum	in bono
	post peccatum, non liberum velle bonum	qua bonum volumus	qua bonum ipsum affectuose volumus

Lam suggests that Gilbert uses St Augustine for his theology of original sin, grace and liberty, and predestination, 'Gilbert of Hoyland' in DSp 6 (1967) 373; Lam finds Gilbert faithful to the thought of Bernard, while changing Bernard's words; see *Sancti Bernardi Opera,* ed. J. Leclercq, H. M. Rochais, (Rome: Ed. Cistercienses, 1963) 3:165-203, *De gratia et libero arbitrio,* and *S. Anselmi Opera Omnia,* ed. F. S. Schmitt, (Edinburgh: Nelson 1946) 1:205-226, *De libertate arbitrii*; see index below (volume 4) under 'choice' and 'liberty'.

2.   Probably S 38:5-6; see also 35:2, 7. For 'rudiments of formation', Lam cites 'vigils, fasts, a modest and sparce diet, rough cloth, black bread and strokes of the discipline freely undertaken', S 43:8. Lam 170, nn. 3, 4; 174, n. 22.

3.   Lam, 'Gilbert de Hoyland', DSp 6 (1967) 372-3.

4.   For such an interpretation, à Lapide, 8:85, quotes Anselm and refers to Richard of St Victor.

SERMON 40
CONTINENCE, REPENTANCE,
AND ALL VIRTUES

The bride bears the fruit of continence, repentance, and of all the virtues. 1. Gilbert's humble confession. 2. False love forgets the absent lover and courts the present, but true love does not act so. 3. Fears for the loss of virginity. 4. The Lord is a passionate lover. 5. He invites from the bride's garden of activity to his own of contemplation. 6. The mystical meanings of myrrh in Christ; chastity differs in Christ, Mary and others; St Lawrence is invited from the gridiron to the garden. 7. Christ's Resurrection is the promise of our own. 8. His Godhead in the flesh is like honey in the honeycomb; gall and vinegar become as sweet as milk and honey.

LET MY BELOVED COME INTO HIS GARDEN TO EAT THE FRUIT OF HIS ORCHARD. COME INTO MY GARDEN, SISTER, MY BRIDE. I HAVE GATHERED MY MYRRH WITH MY SPICES. I HAVE EATEN THE HONEYCOMB WITH MY HONEY; I HAVE DRUNK MY WINE WITH MY MILK*[1]

Sg 5:1

W hat a gulf exists, brethren, between my behavior and the words which express such desires. The Lord knows my eagerness but I am not rash. Why not be rash? I have no such garden as Christ pictured above, no apples which he eagerly consumes, no fragrant fruits, no gushing fountain, no deep well of living waters. But rather into my garden burst quickly thorns and brambles. *I do not dare, good Jesus, to invite you into such a garden, unless perhaps first to weed, harrow and scatter, and then to plant, and thus in due season you will eat from what your right hand has planted.*[*2]

Ps 79:16

Happy the soul worthy to invite you to fruit already ripe, cultivated fruit without bitterness. Would that bitterness were the only complaint about our fruits! would that they were only unripe, provided they were not bad! Often apples which by nature are good, are not yet tasty because of the season and are only distasteful because unripe. Happy the garden in which all fruits are both good by nature and ready in season. The bride knows that neither quality is lacking in her apples, for to partake of them she entices her Beloved. 'Let my Beloved come into his garden to eat the fruit of his orchard.'

See with what hesitation and modesty and after how many eulogies was her invitation extended. Indeed she does not presume to invite her Beloved, nor does she thirst for delights, until she knows she has been described in quite delicate terms. What do you conclude? Do you think that Jesus grants the delightful coming of his presence to those neither endowed with the qualities mentioned nor worthy of his praises? Consider it a mark of rash presumption to invite Jesus before you are ready for the practise of contemplation. Do you pester him to dally with you, when perhaps you are still grubby with faults? Is your garden still prickly with brambles and becoming barren? And do you invite Jesus there? Invite him not now to dally but to destroy what your right hand has planted. Invite him first to uproot and then to plant. In both there is toil, but with delight he will come to pluck ripe fruit.

2. 'Let my Beloved come,' she cries. Not only does she woo and compliment him in his presence but even in his absence her longing for him is fervent. A false and counterfeit love forgets someone absent but woos someone present. Not so does his bride act,

not so; she longs for him in his absence and rejoices in his presence. 'Let my Beloved come into his garden,' she says. Why does he dispatch the south wind to me? Let him come in person and it is enough for me. He is my south wind, he is my fragrance. He is my south wind, he is my love. 'God comes from the south'* and the south wind comes with him.   *Heb 3:3*

According to John, 'he is full of grace and truth'.*   *Jn 1:14* Rightly is he my south wind, for he scatters the clouds with his light and gently approaches. My south wind is my Christ. He blows through my garden, he eats my apples. 'Let my Beloved come into his garden, to eat the fruit of his orchard.' The time for pruning has passed; the blossom has given birth to fruit with which it was in labor; winter is gone, spring has vanished, early autumn treads on the heels of departing summer. At last 'let my Beloved come into his garden to eat the fruit of his orchard'. Behold the fulness of time has now come;* therefore 'let my   *Ga 4:4* Beloved come into his garden'. The apples have ripened early, therefore 'let him eat the fruit of his orchard.

He longs for the first-fruits of the fig tree. Though it was not yet time for figs, he approached a fig tree by the wayside, turned its leaves over and found no fruit.* Before the time for eating and before the time   *Mk 11:13* for fruit, he approached it in the morning hungry. For my part I know a fig tree which bore morning fruit from its first childhood, a harvest of firstfruits, fruits of virginal grace. This fig tree was not planted by the wayside but in a garden and in a garden enclosed, in a garden surrounded by the wall of discipline and the thick hedge of custody. Obviously fruitful was this fig tree and among others the most beautiful in appearance. The Lord Jesus often turned aside to it, perhaps adapting her words: 'Beneath the shade of one whom I desired, I sat and the fruit was sweet to my palate.'[3]

3. But would that the tree had kept the fruits it produced! Would that the wicked hand of a thief had not deflowered the tree! Now however it has borne its best fruit, and fruit which cannot be reborn. Other

fruit has grown in its place, that is, instead of virginal
continence, bitter repentance. With how much greater
relish you used to feed both yourself and your
Beloved on that natural fruit rather than on this sub-
stitute! Woe to you in your misery! When your
Beloved shall come, what will be your thoughts,
your appearance, your countenance? Where will you
turn in your shame, after you have lost the fruits of
modesty? Where will you turn? When he shall
approach and turn over your leaves and not find the
usual fruit, he will blush at your confusion! Recall
the words of the vow of virginity; review the words
of your consecration. Wait beneath the foliage, since
your special fruit no longer exists, the fruit of
integrity, the fruit of virginity. Such fruit was con-
secrated but now it has been plucked.

Consecration and corruption do not sit well together. Violated virginity is wont to be forgiven,
though it cannot be given back. 'Glorious tales have
been sung about you, O city of God',* but shameful
deeds have been done within you. In future, in
lamentation acknowledge your role with twofold
confusion and shame. 'Who will give water to my
head and a fountain of tears to my eyes, and I shall
weep'* for the fall not of some woman of the street
but as it were, of the foremost in the virginal flock?[4]
Who I ask will give me 'a fountain of tears'? For she
who has fallen has been wholly dissolved in tears;
streams of tears roll down and drench her face. Deep
sighs and fretful moans betray what shame, the faithful companion of guilt, tries to hide. In her pitiful
face I have seen her downcast look, her furrowed
cheeks. Sobs interrupted her words; she would not
refrain from falling and could not refrain from tears.

Produce what you are producing, 'the appropriate
fruits of repentance'.* Let sorrow renew you; be
consumed by grief;* say with the prophet: 'Do not
try to console me, I shall weep bitterly.'* I also shall
weep with you. Perhaps your Beloved in person will
also shed tears with you, since he wept for Lazarus.*
Perhaps he weeps even more. His grief is greater, for
his love is greater. His mercies are many; 'therefore,'

Ps 86:3.
Lam 17, n. 68.

Jr 9:11

Lk 3:8
Dt 28:65
Is 22:4

Jn 11:35

says the prophet, 'we have not been consumed.'* *Lm 3:22*
In scriptural terms, you are not consumed because he
is your counsellor and your consoler, converting
your soul.* *Is 9:6; Jb 29:25; Ps 22:3*

To say what almost defies understanding, how
will the pitiful face of your grief fail to move his
feelings, though in a different way, when I who
retrace the course of your sorrow am touched
inwardly with heartfelt compassion? If you produce
'the appropriate fruits of repentance', your Beloved
will return again into his garden. Yes, gladly he consumes the apples of repentance. Blessed, however, is
anyone who guards intact the fruit of original purity.
It is good to come to maturity early and in maturity
to persevere.

4. Therefore the Bride rises before dawn[5] and
says: 'Let my Beloved come into his garden to eat his
fruit of his orchard.' 'Come into my garden, sister,
my bride.' A passionate lover is the Lord Jesus; at a
single word of invitation, he comes flying gladly into
the bride's little garden. He flies ahead, as it were, and
'rising before dawn,' cries 'Come'![6] Let this word be
taken as an imperative and his cry 'Come!' will suit
his actions. He is no dilatory or niggardly rewarder,
but without restraint repeats the bride's invitation:
'Come into my garden, sister, my bride. I have
gathered my myrrh with my spices.' It is an obdurate
affection, which is not moved by such tender invitations and reinvitations! What is more gracious than
this interchange? What more surprising than this
exchange?

Oh wonderful exchange! The Beloved of God the
Father, the glory of heaven, the delight of the angels,
allows himself to be invited into our little gardens
and does not neglect to invite us to his in return.
Even the garden which is ours is more truly called
his. For the bride does not say: 'let my Beloved
come into *my* garden' but 'into *his* garden'. Rightly
'into his', because given by him and owed to him and
certainly dedicated to him. 'Let my Beloved come.'
'Come, sister, my bride.' Great is their tenderness
and apt their distinctions. She desires and he

commands. She says: 'Let him come'; he answers,
'Come!'

Rv 3:20
'I stand at the door and knock,' he says. 'If anyone opens to me, I will enter and dine with him and
he with me.'* *You have no need to linger, O good
Jesus, at the door of the bride, for on her own
initiative in her yearning she anticœpates you. Reply
in kind, invite her in turn. You have sat at her table;
notice the quantities set before you, knowing you
should prepare for her a repast to match. A repast
to match I suggest, and it is enough for her. But I
assure you of this: she expends herself without
reserve; you should respond in kind. How will it be
in kind, if she gives herself fully and you give only
half of yourself? A mite of yourself is more than
her all. Her all is but a share of your grace; that is
why her garden is yours and your garden is hers.*

5. 'Come into my garden.' For my part, brethren,
gladly I see in the Bridegroom's garden that abundant and delicate and gloriously planted paradise of
Christ's virtues which, in accord with his two natures,
he either possessed from eternity or received in time.
So, in a parallel, see in the bride's garden the state of
the soul or of the Church and the dowry of virtues
and affections with which each is enriched by the
Bridegroom. In her garden are considered the blessings of the Body, in his garden the blessings of the
Head. In both there is beautiful fruit for contemplation. But what is her fruit compared with his? The
more the glory of Christ surpasses the virtues either
of the soul or of the Church, so much the more
delightful is the entrance into his garden.

The active life looks more to the bride's garden,
contemplation alone looks to his. Although the bride
rejoices over her garden, she takes pains with it and
in the sweat of her brow she feeds on her fruit; when
she is led into his garden, nothing remains but delight
alone. She guards her own garden but gazes upon
his. Nor is she led into his garden except from her
own, that is, from activity to the practice of contemplation. Or, if we admit contemplation into the
garden of the bride, it resembles activity. Yes, from

her many activities in due order one comes to his
myrrh. Only with abundance of virtues will she enter
the garden of her Beloved.

'You will enter the tomb with abundance,' says
Job.* Here, of course, 'the garden' sounds better than   *Jb 5:26*
'the tomb'. The tomb suggests repose and some
retreat from cares; the garden expresses a vision
and a banquet. In the tomb we have leisure; in the
garden we have pleasure. Now just as we enter the
tomb only with abundance, as Job says, much more
so do we enter the garden. Therefore the Bridegroom invites the bride from her garden to his
garden: 'Come into my garden, sister, my bride.'
Enter, my bride, enter into the contemplation of the
virtues of your Beloved, enter into his delights,
remember only his justice. There God, your God, will
teach you in joyfulness and his right hand will escort
you wonderfully.* He will feed you with the fruit of   *Ps 44:5*
life and understanding. Myrrh and spices he has
harvested for you.

6. 'I have gathered my myrrh with my spices,'
he says. Immortality and incorruptibility indeed he
gathered after death. Thanks to myrrh, of course,
bodies of the dead are preserved unharmed. 'Myrrh,'
says the Bridegroom, 'which is mine.' Truly it is his,
since he was the first to receive it and is the only one
to share it. For the firstfruits are Christ and then
those who belong to him. Through him is the
resurrection of the dead, for being the first to rise
'he dies no more'.* Good is such myrrh and better   *Rm 6:9*
than the myrrh we use; ours prevents dead flesh from
decaying, but his myrrh does not permit flesh to fail
once it is restored to life. His myrrh was also his
peerless and unique virginal chastity, which neither
felt the first flicker nor possessed the tinder of
wantonness. In him neither was such a flicker
extinguished nor its tinder removed, for this was
anticipated with anointings of myrrh, yes, of his own
myrrh. The myrrh of others is effective and its em-
balming goes only so far as to preserve from corruption; but his myrrh keeps the Lord's flesh untouched
by corruptibility.

The myrrh of others follows on the corruption of carnal provocation; his myrrh prevents all provocation. Theirs excludes; his precludes. In Jesus there is neither corruption nor its cause. In his Mother, though there be its cause, still there is no corruption. In all others there is both corruption and its cause. Our myrrh represses the rising movements of carnal concupiscence. Mary's myrrh knew nothing of such movements. Jesus' myrrh had neither the cause nor the beginning of being so moved. 'Of his fullness we have all received'* and myrrh from his myrrh. The myrrh of our chastity is from the gift and the imitation of himself; therefore when he harvests myrrh in us he is harvesting his own myrrh. May he find much myrrh in me to harvest!

Jo 1:10

'Myrrh with spices', means either absention from evil with aspirations for goodness, or austerity of the flesh and devotion of the heart. Whether we mean moderation in what is lawful or endurance of injuries, in myrrh the spices of both virtues are well blended. This myrrh is indeed a grace, if we are scourged when we do good or if, afflicting ourselves outwardly, we are thereby affected with inner consolation.

Abundant myrrh the Lord harvested from the field of the martyr Lawrence, whose feast we are now celebrating, and abundant spices: the myrrh of confession, the spices of confession. Delivered to the flames, he indeed confessed Christ; he gave up his body to be burned, he distributed his possessions to the poor.[7] His flesh was consumed by fire for Christ, but his heart was consumed by a greater fire in Christ. Therefore from the gridiron he is invited to the garden. Even while he was on the gridiron, he was not absent from the garden. Now he is only in the garden, yet not wholly in it. His flesh is still bound in corruption; it has not yet blossomed anew. It will blossom anew, however, when our lowly body is conformed to the glorified body of Jesus.

Then our lowly body will harvest the myrrh of immortality and the spices of manifold glory which Jesus harvested beforehand. Then assuredly Jesus will proclaim his invitation: 'Come into my garden, sister,

my bride.' Then he will boast of a full harvest of
myrrh with his spices. For then he will gather the
result of his Passion and of his prayers, which are
signified by the spices. 'Offering up prayers with a
loud cry and with tears, . . . he was heard because of
his reverence . . . and became the source of eternal
salvation to all who obey him.'[8] 'I desire,' he says,
that 'where I am, there also my servant may be.'*   *Jn 12:26*
Where, but in his garden? We shall be in his garden,
at the fulness of the general resurrection; yet even
now, we are in his garden through contemplation.

7. For we enter into his garden, as it were, when
with affection, respect and longing, we consider what
we shall be like through him and what he has already
become for us at his Resurrection and as an example
for us. Why do I say at his Resurrection? Even before
his Resurrection, his whole way of life displays the
charm of a very beautiful garden; but what he
planted beforehand, later he reaped. At our resurrection is the time of ripeness and of reaping, when each
will receive the fruit of his labors. Thus his calling us
into his garden, his adding that he has harvested his
myrrh with his spices, encourages us to contemplate
the glory of the resurrection which is to come for us
through him or which has already preceded in him
for us.

Is it not a joyful and truly delightful progress to
enter Christ's garden, to enter the Lord's plantation,
by gazing on him virtue by virtue? 'Gazing,' I say, for
I dare not say approaching. For who promises himself an approach to the reality and fulness of his
virtues? Pleasant indeed is this digression and surely
profitable. Nowhere else is the haughtiness of the
human mind better checked by humiliation, or its
hunger more satisfied by contemplation, or its dis-
taste more tempted by emulation. The comparison is
humiliating; the imitation is stimulating; the consideration is delightful. The first overwhelms; the second
challenges; the third nourishes. His immensity overwhelms; his righteousness challenges; his truth
nourishes.*   *Lam 198, n. 183.*

8. A little later in the Canticle, the Beloved

Sg 5:1

himself, the Bridegroom himself invites his friends
and his most beloved to eat and drink and be
inebriated.* In order that a greater appetite may be
born in them, he first woos them by mentioning one
course from his own menu: 'I have eaten the honeycomb with my honey.' *Both are yours, good Jesus,
the honey you give and the honey you are. But in
this place the honey which you are yourself pours
more readily into our understanding. Why do you not
say 'your' honeycomb, as you say 'your' honey? Why
do you now resort to this distinction? The honeycomb is also 'yours' as the honey is 'yours', although
you openly claim 'your' honey and fail to proclaim
'your' honeycomb. Each of two natures is 'yours', but
the divine is 'yours' and, as it were, naturally 'yours',
while the human is not as it were 'naturally yours',
but rather assumed and made 'natural to you'
through your kindness to us.*

'I have eaten the honeycomb with my honey.'
Before being conceived by the holy Virgin, the Godhead not yet incarnate existed, as it were, as Honey
alone without the honeycomb. Afterwards the honey
existed in the honeycomb, God in man. Now, however, the honeycomb exists in the honey, man
clothed in Godhead. 'And if we have known Christ
according to the flesh, now we no longer know him

2 Co 5:16

so', says the apostle.* As God was concealed in the
flesh, so now conversely his flesh has been hidden in
God. Although that flesh has been glorified, so that
it is now spiritual and has nothing of infirmity, still
the flesh is somehow hidden while we await and
adore him instead in as much as he is God. Somehow
the honeycomb of his flesh is concealed in the honey
of the Godhead, while our reverence for his revealed
majesty completely absorbs our wonder and our faith.

At last, then, after the glory of his Resurrection,
Christ consumes the honeycomb with his honey, and
without the indignity of fleshly infirmity in the substance of the flesh he assumed, he enjoys a delight
divine and natural to him exclusively. 'I have eaten
the honeycomb with my honey; I have drunk my
wine with my milk.' Now you speak of both as

'yours', both milk and wine. Yours are the rights of each nature, the properties of each nature, without the faults of humanity; and just as he drinks new wine, so also he drinks new milk. 'With my milk,' he says, that is with the milk of your newness, not of our infirmity.

9. Run, O bride, hasten to so sweet a banquet, where the wine, where the milk belong to the Bridegroom, where the honeycomb is not empty, not void, but filled with honey. 'Honey you have found; consume what is sufficient,'* for you are not sufficient for it all. Jesus himself, however, does not consume in measure but consumes the whole, for he is sufficient for the whole. This advice is given to you: 'Do not search into majesty lest you be overwhelmed by its glory',* but he searches all things even the depths of God.* No one knows the Father but the Son and he to whom the Son wills to reveal him.* He consumes the whole, he shares a part with whom he wills and as much as he wills. He promises you, as it were, a sharing in this food, glorying that he has been refreshed.

Pr 25:16

Ps 25:27
1 Co 2:10

Mt 11:27

If for your food you have been given gall, if in your thirst you have drunk vinegar, remember that Jesus suffered the like. These he tasted on the Cross but did not drink,* so suggesting the swift passage of bitterness. But he drinks wine with his milk. No longer is he distressed at the tomb for Lazarus, no longer is he sad unto death; he does not drink vinegar and gall at the point of death. The old have passed away; the new have come instead. The distress, sadness and boredom, inherited for a time from the old man in the economy of salvation, have passed into the new sweetness of milk.* Good is the wine if, when you drink of it, bygone tortures are consigned to oblivion and do not overwhelm your heart. Instead the heart is regaled with new, pure and milk-white affections in the flesh now restored to life, while at last for the future, unlike the past, no insult, no trial is either assumed or endured, either in soul or body; but the vinegar mixed with gall, which he tasted without drinking, has passed into

Mt 27:34

Lam 198, n. 182.

the savor of wine and milk.

Do you also, O faithful soul, who enjoy the dignity of the bride, be confident that this change will be yours. He proclaims that these changes have been completed in himself precisely that you may learn to hope for the like in yourself. Indeed he wishes to banquet with you, to drink with you: 'I will not drink of this fruit of the vine,' he says, 'until I drink it anew in my kingdom'.* This kingdom he points out to you, when he calls you to the garden, to the garden of delights, the paradise of pleasure, to the ripe fruits, to the fruits already plucked by him and to be plucked by you. Then you will drink wine with milk, that you may forget bygone torture and taste the sweetness of the new resurrection, thanks to our Lord, who lives and reigns for ever and ever. Amen.

Mt 26:29

NOTES TO SERMON FORTY

1.   G. speaks to *fratres* in par. 1 and 5, on the Feast of St Lawrence, probably 10 August 1166; G. addresses the bride in the second person singular, but also a reader or correspondent.

2.   Compare the end of par. 1. Lam 183, n. 86.

3.   Sg 2:3; G. adapts the bride's words for the Bridegroom; reading *quam* with mss Paris 9605, Troyes 419, for *quem* of Mab. and Migne; G. refers to the Church.

4.   This foremost of the virginal flock, who after a fall produces fruits of repentance, would have been a contemporary of the nun of Watton. Aelred of Rievaulx relates the story, PL 195: 789-95. See Powicke, lxxxi-lxxxii and Squire, 117-8; the latter set the date at about 1160. Mikkers, 39, suggested that this sermon may have been delivered to nuns, not to monks. See L. Braceland, 'Nuns in the Audience of Gilbert of Hoyland', forthcoming article in the pages of the 1976 Kalamazoo Cistercian Studies Conference.

5.   Ps 118:147, *praevenit in maturitate;* the homonym is lost in English.

6.   Translating *Veni,* as imperative with G., not perfect indicative.

7.   1 Co 13:3. Lam 171, n. 8, finds liturgical texts in par. 4 and 6.

8.   Heb 5:7, 9; reading *factus omnibus obtemperantibus* with mss and Migne for *omnino* of Mab.

SERMON 41
MILK, HONEY, AND WINE

The bride is invited to a banquet with milk, honey, and wine. 1. The primitive Church was happily ready for harvest. 2. The Bridegroom waits to reap all he has sown. 3. When will we be ready for his call? 4. Aelred was ready: a full sheaf, abundant myrrh, and an overflowing honeycomb. 5. We should have well-built honeycombs waiting to be filled with the honey of heavenly hope. 6. Aelred blended milk and wine which went to the heads of his hearers. 7. Aelred, once our help and now our honor, enjoys the banquet we shall all enjoy after the universal resurrection. 8. Cherish this hope of the resurrection when friends will become most dearly beloved. 9. With charity above all, we are called from fleeting joy here to inebriating joy hereafter.

I HAVE GATHERED MY MYRRH WITH MY SPICES, I HAVE EATEN THE HONEYCOMB WITH MY HONEY, I HAVE DRUNK MY WINE WITH MY MILK. EAT FRIENDS AND DRINK AND BE INEBRIATED MOST DEARLY LOVED*[1]   *Sg 5:1*

'I have gathered my myrrh with my spices, I have eaten the honeycomb with my honey, I have drunk my wine with my milk. Come into my garden, sister, my bride.' Take it, brethren, that this call refers to the end of the world, when with all the mysteries of the Church accomplished, she is

491

Mt 13:39
Jo 4:35

called to the kingdom, when the Lord will send his
harvesting angels* because her realms will then be
white for the harvest.* Oh happy the times of the
primitive Church! How fruitful then was her field,
what abundant harvests it produced! What mellow-
ness of myrrh there was in her martyrs! How many
bees were building the honeycombs of a more perfect
and mystic doctrine! One might think amid the very
beginnings of the faith, when the seeds of the word
were being sown, that it was already harvest time and
that her realms were growing white, ripe for the sickle.
*Why do you delay, good Jesus? Why not call the
bride into your garden? Can you not already say:
'I have gathered my myrrh with my spices, I have
eaten the honeycomb with my honey, I have drunk
my wine with my milk'?*

Where now are the martyrs in the myrrh, where
are the doctors in the honeycomb, where are the
fervent spirits denoted by the wine and those
innocent of evil symbolized by the sweetness of
milk? Does not the field of your Church now seem
stripped of such glory? Have you multiplied the
Is 9:3
nation without increasing its joy?* Many are the
harvests of believers but few their spices. Autumn
fruitfulness preceded in those first days of the
nascent Church; now stark winter oppresses us. The
years of fruitfulness preceded; now years of barrenness brood over us. After the plump and festive ears
Gn 41:6
of corn, spindly and blighted ears appear.* *Why do
you not cry at last, good Jesus, 'Come into my
garden, sister, my bride'? Why wait? Why add delay
upon delay? Is it that after this winter autumn
may return?*

'They will rejoice again in your presence, as men
Is 9:3
rejoice at the harvest.'* 'Then you will bless the
crown of the year with your bounty and your fields
Ps 64:12
Ps 64:3
will be filled with abundance.'* 'The pastures of'
what now seems our 'wilderness, will be luxuriant',*
and the rage of the most recent persecution will
bring to our harvests the gleaming whiteness of
maturity. 'They will be multiplied' in an old age not
faltering, not wasted, not barren, but 'in a ripe old

age; rightly shall they be patient that they may be
heralds',* patient through martyrdom, heralds
through the word! In the patient you will reap
myrrh; in heralds you will eat the honeycomb. Then
you will toast your elect in the wine of compunction, blended with the milk of consolation. For unless
the Lord had shortened those days, no flesh could
survive.*

Ps 91:15-16

Mt 24:22

2. Even now the Lord reaps, although not as
much as myrrh as then, yet much myrrh of voluntary
penance. He eats the honeycomb with honey and
when the sweetness of the spiritual meaning has been
extracted, he makes us delight in the figures which
contain it. He drinks wine with milk, because he
tempers and sweetens lofty meanings and surpassing
contemplations with the simplicity of faith and
morals. He loves the fervor of zeal, provided milk is
at hand to nourish the little ones.[2] When all our
resources have been distributed, when the eras of the
martyrs have passed away, when teachers like honeycombs containing wisdom hidden in mystery,* have
completed their ministry and under pressure from
the arguments of heretics have poured forth honeyed
doctrine, when the babes who are nourished with
milk and the fervent in spirit, inebriated with the
wine of grace and forgetting what lies behind,* have
completed their numbers and their days, when all this
has been accomplished; 'for not one iota or one cir-
cumflex of the Law shall disappear until all is
accomplished',* then the whole Church of the saints
will exult at this invitation so gracious: 'Come into
my garden, sister, my bride. I have gathered my
myrrh with my spices, I have eaten the honeycomb
with my honey, I have drunk my wine with my
milk.'

1 Co 2:7

Ph 3:13

*Mt 5:18. See Lam
6, n. 6; 7,
nn. 16, 19.*

'I have gathered, eaten, drunk'; these verbs in the
past tense denote total fulfillment, as if one should
say: 'It has been accomplished.'* 'Come into my
garden, sister, my bride. I have gathered my myrrh
with my spices.' 'Come into my garden', where no
nettle springs up hard by to grieve the grace of the
lilies, where sharp thorns do not pierce the blossom-

Jn 19:30

ing rose, where no tree exists to which access is forbidden. 'Come into my garden, sister, my bride. I have gathered my myrrh with my spices.'

Hear how he harvests only what is his own, only what he himself has previously sown. Truly he is a wicked and lazy servant, who by a malicious interpretation abuses his master to excuse his own laziness: 'I know that you are a hard man, plucking what you did not plant and reaping where you did not sow.'*

Mt 25:24

Truly lazy is he, for in him his lord found nothing to reap, and truly wicked for by a perverse interpretation he construed as harshness the thrifty gleaning of his master, hoarding without interest what he had received and forming an insulting opinion of a good lord. The Lord Jesus reaps only what he has sown, reaps only what is his own. What an enemy sows over his wheat, he does not reap but will send angels to gather the cockle and to bundle it for burning, for they glean all scandals from his kingdom.*[3] There-

Mt 13:24-30, 37-42

fore he first purges his kingdom of scandals, his field from cockle and his garden from useless plants, that he may reap and bundle only what is his own.

3. If Jesus were to arrive now, if the angel's voice were to ring out, if the last trumpet were to sound its terrifying blast, if the court were assembled, 'fire enkindled in his presence', heaven summoned from above and earth 'to separate his people',* if now all

Ps 49:3-4

this were suddenly to catch you off guard, what opinion would you have of your merits? In your own judgement, where should you be stationed? Among his saints who will be assembled there, or among those who will be assembled in the binding of one bundle for the pit? Amid the cockle or amid the spices? Does even your own judgement of yourself perhaps waver? Who will boast that he has no cockle in his field? Happy the man in whom there is but a little and that not cultivated, not irrigated, but hiding and lurking in some supply of spices and to be uprooted from the garden as soon as one notices it.

Woe to me, O Lord, for my imperfection, if you are a hard man, if you are a harsh creditor, if you 'pluck what you did not plant and harvest where

*you did not sow'!** Woe to me, if you reap all you*   Mt 25:24
sowed, without forgiveness and regard for devotion!
For not all you sowed in me has grown up. May you
deign to accept the bundle of my myrrh, that it may
*rest between your breasts.** May the incense from my*   Sg 1:12
*spices, barely visible, ascend to you.**   Js 4:15

    But when shall I offer you a comb full of
honey? When shall I offer you a constant meditation
*on your Law?** when a pure and full understanding of*   Ps 118:77
*spiritual mysteries?** when the honeyed wisdom Paul*   1 Co 12:1
mentions among the perfect? For as the honey of the   1 Co 2:6
honeycomb is contained in cells, so heavenly wisdom
is contained in the purest mysteries of symbols, that
by comparison with each other the truth symbolized
may vouch for the mysteries and truth itself, ex-
tracted as it were from such cells, may attract no
little grace.[4] *When shall I be able to mix for you that*
blend of wine and milk in some mixing-bowl of my
heart? This is a rare blend, that one who is carried
*out of his mind to God should learn to be sober,**   2 Co 5:13
that while acquainted with sublime truths he may
*sympathize with the lowly,** and while intoxicated*   Rm 12:16
*with a purer understanding he may become a babe.**   1 Th 2:7

    4. How great a honeycomb, how vast and how
rich, has been transferred in these days to the
heavenly banquet! I mean the Lord Abbot of Rievaulx, whose passing was announced to us while we
were treating of this verse. It seems to me that by his
having been taken from us, our garden has been
stripped and has consigned a large bundle of myrrh
to God, its cultivator. No similar honeycomb is left
in our apiary. In him could be seen both a honeycomb
and a bundle of myrrh with good spices. Who was
purer in life or more prudent in teaching than he?
Who was more sickly in the flesh or more hearty in
spirit than he? His speech like a honeycomb poured
out honeyed knowledge.[5] Pining in the flesh, interiorly in spirit he pined still more with love of
things heavenly. With his flesh all myrrh, his mind all
spices, with continual burning he offered the sweet-
smelling incense of unflagging love. In a body drained
and withered, 'his soul was fed as with marrow and

Ps 62:6
Sg 4:11

fat'. Therefore 'with exultant lips his mouth will ever praise the Lord',* for his 'lips are a distilling honeycomb'.* For wholly changed into lips by his modest countenance and the tranquil bearing of his whole body, he betrayed the calm affections of his spirit. He was lucid in interpretation, not hasty in speech. He questioned modestly, replied more modestly, tolerating the troublesome, himself troublesome to no one. Acutely intelligent, deliberate in statement, he bore annoyance with equanimity. I remember how often when someone of his audience rudely interrupted the course of his instruction, he stopped speaking until the other had fully exhausted his breath; when the gushing torrent of untimely speech had ebbed away, he would resume his interrupted discourse with the same calmness with which he had waited, for he both spoke and kept silent as the occasion demanded.* Quick to listen, slow to speak, but not slow to anger.* How is he to be described as slow to anger? I would rather say he was not in the race!

2 T 4:2
Jm 1:19

5. Truly he was a honeycomb, because fully designed and built of clear cells, in every act, word and gesture he was thought to distill a honey of inner sweetness. Happy was he, for in him Jesus found a full honeycomb to eat, bulging not extracted. Consider the nature of a honeycomb: its head is, as it were, helmeted from the shape of the hive in which it is born. Then it hangs from the top and extends from the top. The hope of eternal salvation is a good helmet according to Paul.* From the hope of things above, the principle of all actions and the purpose of all life together should begin; they should cling to hope, aim at hope and by hope defend themselves against all temptations. If you should see a man who, thanks to his hope in things above, in every act, even in adversity, is filled with a spiritual joy sweeter than honey,* what should you consider him but a honeycomb, overflowing with honey from every cell?

1 Th 5:8

Si 24:27

If you see a man of sound common sense and orderly behavior, self-consistent in the measured control of his deeds and conduct, fully equipped

with matching cells, but cells empty and drained of
the liquid honey of hope stored in heaven,* does he   *Col 1:5*
suggest to you anything other than the aridity of a
dried up honeycomb? He has a twofold disadvantage,
if at the same time he is both dissipated by distrac-
tion and drained by lack of devotion. Yet it is one
thing, if he keeps up appearances to counterfeit virtue, and quite another thing, if he appears as a
honeycomb with cells designed in the good hope that
grace may be poured in, so that he may not lack a
container fashioned for the gift of spiritual sweetness
and cells ideal for honey from above.

6. But this honeycomb of ours which we are discussing was full to overflowing with interior liquid. It
was full of cells; on either side it dripped sweetness.
As a busy bee he fashioned the honeycombs of the
divine word. Good are the honeycombs from which,
while they remain intact, the mouths of many are
daily sweetened. He did not search out some tasteless
subtlety which provides matter for wrangling rather
than instruction. Busy to gather a knowledge of
morals, he stored it in the well-fashioned cells of his
words. He was prudent in mystical discourse which
he reserved for the perfect.[6] He abounded in milk-
clear teaching for the salvation and consolation of
little ones, yet he often slyly mixed with it the wine
of a merry and sparkling diction. This is the truth.
His milk was as potent as wine. His simple teaching
and milk-clear exposition often swept his listener's
spirit unaware into the intoxicating transport of a
mind beside itself.[7] Hence one addicted to this drink
could rightly say: 'I have drunk wine with milk.'
Indeed he knew how to mix wine deftly in milk and
to dispense either one in the other. He chose material
easy to work with but you could feel in his words the
passion of inebriating grace. He was endowed with a
ready understanding but a passionate affection!

7. We must grieve that recourse to so great a man
has been withdrawn from us; but none the less we
must take pride that we have forwarded such a
bundle of myrrh from our little gardens to the
heavenly garden. He who here was our help, there is

our honor. And if our apiary seems deserted and our garden stripped, yet he left many sheaves from which God is well able to create bundles of increase in virtue.* God does this in the whole Church also, until through succeeding generations, when all ranks have their complement, he may say to his bride now perfect and complete: 'Come into my garden, sister, my bride. I have gathered my myrrh with my spices, I have eaten the honeycomb with my honey, I have drunk my wine with my milk. Eat friends and drink and be inebriated most dearly loved.'

Now in its most perfect realization this is hoped for at the general welcome of the Church into the joy of the Lord, which will take place after the resurrection. Yet we believe that the angelic citizens of heaven are daily invited to a banquet of thanksgiving, when any holy soul, either such as we have recalled above or one of lesser perfection and grace, is transferred into the loveliness of paradise, into gardens ever green, 'into the site of his marvellous tabernacle, even into the home of God'.*

8. Cherish these truths, brethren, remember them and pour out your souls within you. The memory of these truths is a fire; it will make your soul melt and be dissolved into delights and desires, when you pass 'to the site of the marvellous tabernacle'. 'For the outcry of the banqueter is accompanied by songs of exultation and confession.'* There both songs are melodious, the song of the friend who dines and the song of the Lord, his host. For this is the call of our host: 'Eat, friends, and drink and be inebriated, most dearly loved.' 'Friends', he says, and 'most dearly loved'. These are titles of courtship, but his courtship has no taste of flattery; it is full of dedication and love. And these titles of courtship uttered by the Lord do not fail to inebriate; they are able to woo the affections of his guests. Yet each term differs from the other and *most dearly loved* implies greater favor than *friends.* 'You are my friends,' said the Lord to the apostles, 'if you do what I command you. No longer will I call you servants but friends, because I have made known to you all that

I heard from my Father.'*   *Jn 15:14-15*

Here also notice a distinction. In both sentences
the apostles are called friends, but with a difference:
in one because they act, in the other because they
know; in one thanks to their ministry, in the other
thanks to a mystery; in one they eat, in the other they
also drink. In both texts they are friends but not yet
most dearly loved. Intoxication enters the drink of
the most dearly loved. The very form of address
cryptically implies a superabundance and means the
fulness of charity. One most dearly loved is utterly
full of love. One is most dearly loved who is seeped
and drenched in love, whose marrow and bones and
entire inner being are immersed in streams of love.
One is not intoxicated because he is most dearly
loved but one is most dearly loved because he is
intoxicated.

In our text, what else does it mean to be
inebriated but to be filled with the delight of most
perfect love? Perhaps we prefer the following distinction: the most dearly loved are those who love most
fully; the inebriated are those most perfectly filled
with delight. 'Eat, friends, and drink and be inebriated, most dearly loved.' The friends are they who
either act or hearken; the most dearly loved those
who cling fast. Friends act for him and hear from
him; the most dearly loved are inebriated with him.
Friends are they to whom he has communicated
what he heard from the Father; the most dearly loved
are they into whom he has poured full knowledge of
the Father himself. There to friends many things are
taught, here by the most dearly loved one thing is
loved. Among the most dearly loved there is no ex-
pansion of works or teaching but only diffusion and
fulness of love. Friends are they who are in harmony
with the divine will; the most dearly loved are they
who are inebriated and immersed in the pleasure
of divine love.

9. 'Eat, friends.' No longer is it said: 'The poor
shall eat and have their fill',* but 'Eat, friends, and be   *Ps 21:27*
inebriated'. How are they poor who are inebriated
with the richness of the Lord's house?* How is there   *Ps 35:9*

poverty where there is plenty? 'Eat, friends, and
drink and be inebriated, most dearly loved.' You are
my friends and my most dearly loved: friends in the
love of fellowship, most dearly loved in that of
espousals. 'Be inebriated, most dearly loved.' I have
brought you into the wine cellar to set charity in
array within you.* Charity is set in array only when
your mind is inebriated with the passion of perfect
love. Charity is set in array only when it is set above
all other affections. Good is the array when love
holds the highest position. Surpassing love creates
those most dearly loved. The most dearly loved are
they in whom nothing is either devoid of charity or
devoted to other business. The array is full when the
passage is made from the rank of dearly loved to that
of most dearly loved. The array is full when nothing
can be added to the fulness of charity.

Sg 2:4

'Eat, friends, and drink and be inebriated, most
dearly loved.' There all are friends and all are most
dearly loved. All are given to drink and all are
inebriated. However it is not so in this vale of tears,
not so; but many are the friends and few the most
dearly loved. Many are given to drink but not all are
inebriated and those who are inebriated return again
to sobriety. For the moment they are carried out of
their minds but then lapse into their usual temperance. They drowse and they are roused; they slumber
and after a while keep watch again. That is why the
bride continues, "I sleep and my heart keeps watch'.*
Yet these watches do not seem to follow sleep but to
accomapny it. May the Lord Jesus grant us in
watches to understand and you to hear suitable
comment on her words, for he lives and reigns God
for ever and ever. Amen.

Sg 5:2

NOTES ON SERMON FORTY-ONE

1.   G. was preparing this text when news arrived of the death of Aelred of Rievaulx which occurred 11 January 1167. G. addresses his brethren throughout, if in par. 5, *videris . . . tibi*, and elsewhere, the singular be translated 'one of you'. In Aelred G. finds his model of Cistercian perfection, a *doctor mellifluus*, the title later to be conferred on Bernard of Clairvaux, and suited to Aelred, the Bernard of the North. Aptly G. takes Aelred's theme of friendship and compares friends with the most dearly beloved. See J. de Guibert, 'Amitié' in DSp 1 (1936) 500-529, esp. 518-22 on Aelred; see also the lengthy article on 'Charité' by many hands in DSp 2 (1953) 507-691, and A. LeBail, 'Aelred', in DSp 1 (1936) 225-234.

2.   On par. 2 and 7, see Lam 10-11, and note 35.

3.   Note the word-play: *non metit illud, sed mittet angelos.*

4.   This a rare reference to one of the modes of understanding mysteries, according to a monk at *Notre Dame des Prairies,* who refers to Vatican I, Session 3, on Catholic Faith, chapter 4, On Faith and Reason: *Ac ratio quidem, fide illustrata, cum sedulo, pie, ac sobrie quaerit, aliquam, Deo dante, mysteriorum intelligentiam eamque fructuosissimam assequitur tum ex eorum, quae naturaliter cognoscit, analogia, tum e mysteriorum ipsorum nexu inter se et cum fine hominis ultimo.* (Denzinger-Baenwaert, 3016; Denzinger-Schonmetzer, ed 32 [1963] older reference 1796).

5.   De Lubac, *Exégèse,* 1:602-3, and note 1: 'Enfin Gilbert de Hoyland nous indique bien comment nous devrons comprendre l'expression même de *doctor mellifluus*; c'est en prononçant l'éloge d'Aelred de Rievaulx, *le second Bernard,* au lendemain de sa mort: "Comme le rayon de miel dans les cellules de la ruche . . . " . '

6.   Quoted in Charles Dumont, 'Experience in the Cistercian Discipline', CSt 10 (1975) 135-8. See also De Lubac, *Exégèse,* 1:614, n. 12.

7.   Aelred's writings appear in English in CF 2, 5, and others to be published. For a fine biography in English see Aelred Squire, *Aelred of Rievaulx* (London: SPCK, 1969) with bibliography at p. 153, and for a further bibliography see Amédée Hallier, *Un Educateur Monastique, Aelred de Rievaulx,* (Paris: Gabalda, 1959) pp. 181-7, trans. by Columban Heaney, *The Monastic Theology of Aelred of Rievaulx: An Experiential Theology,* CS 2 (1969).

SERMON 42
EXCHANGING VISITS

The lover welcomes His visits and visits those who are His. 1. Spiritual love thrives and watches when animal love is anesthetized. 2. Spiritual sleep and watchfulness mean to sleep to the world and to watch in Christ. 3. Good watchmen are the doctors of the Church. 4. How inspiring and persuasive is the voice of Christ! He is the player and the instrument where all is melodious. 5. He hurries to those who heed his voice and his knock. 6. But some distort his word. 7. He praises his bride and counsels her to visit the Gentiles. 8. The ambitious should follow the example of the bride.

I SLEEP AND MY HEART WATCHES. THE VOICE OF MY BELOVED AS HE KNOCKS: 'OPEN TO ME MY SISTER, MY KIN, MY DOVE, MY SPOTLESS ONE, FOR MY HEAD IS MOIST WITH DEW AND MY LOCKS WITH DROPS OF THE NIGHT.' 'I HAVE PUT OFF MY TUNIC; HOW CAN I DON IT AGAIN? I HAVE WASHED MY FEET; HOW CAN I SOIL THEM AGAIN?' MY BELOVED THRUST HIS HAND THROUGH THE LATCH-HOLE AND AT HIS TOUCH MY HEART WAS THRILLED. I AROSE TO OPEN TO MY BELOVED[1]   *Sg 5:2-5*

'I sleep and my heart watches.' What is the logical connection between yesterday's passage and the words which introduce the reply of the bride? Then there was a general invitation; now this is the answer of one person. There many are invited, here one replies. There it is said: 'Be inebriated, most dearly loved'; here she who is most dearly loved because she is the bride, replies that she is asleep: 'I sleep'. Why wonder if a reply in the singular is made to a universal invitation?[2] Many are most dearly loved but all have one heart and one soul. 'My dove', we read, 'is one'.* Love unites and love inebriates. Do you see how rightly one reply is made for all whom the powerful draught of charity pours into a common vessel?[3] Powerful surely is the virtue of love, inebriating and transforming oneself.

Would you hear how charity transforms the spirit it inebriates? 'I sleep', says the bride, as if she were to tell her Beloved: You summon me to inebriation and I am wholly free for your gift. 'I sleep and my heart watches.' I sleep and rest from other pre-occupations; therefore my heart more freely keeps watch to pursue this inebriation and to drink your wine. The sequence is surprising: from inebriation to sleep and from sleep to vigils. He says 'Be inebriated' and she says 'I sleep'. A good slumber is transport of mind, a withdrawal both from sensations of the flesh and (if this also be mentioned) from the senses of the body. Then spiritual love becomes robust and vigilant, when every animal passion and feeling dozes in deep slumber. Both slumber and inebriation, each gives the appearance of withdrawal from oneself. Herein indeed they have a common interrelationship, that inebriation no less than slumber whisks the mind out of itself and dislodges the mind from its home. Each, so to speak, robs the soul itself of its pristine state and informs it with new affections. 'I sleep and my heart watches.'

Some sleep a sleep of their own and their delight reposes in their own self will and pleasure. Far from them do I sleep and my heart keeps vigil for you. After your excoriation, O Lord, others sleep, but I

Sg 6:8

sleep after draining your cup.* Your excoriation is
harsh enough when, disguising your concern, you
leave man to his own indolence, just as your severe
excoriation is a sign of your abandonment.* After
God's excoriation man sleeps, for after God disguises
his concern, man surrenders to a drowsy disinterest;
man does not realize that the patience of God, who
disguises his concern, gives birth to the rejection of
the impenitent. The forbearance of One who is
patient and for the moment does not strike has
power over reverent minds, but the same longsuffering of the Lord which makes upright minds
cautious, makes obdurate minds careless.

2. 'I sleep and my heart watches.' I sleep, not
excoriated but after draining the wine to which you
call your most dearly loved. The drugged wine of
your inebriation withdraws me from the world and
delivers me to you; it makes me sleep and makes me
wake; it makes me forget worldlings and not forget
you. 'I sleep.' Sleep with me for you clearly state[4]
in the words of Solomon: 'If two sleep together,
they will keep each other warm.'* Thus gradually, in
the presence of my Beloved, my heart will be more
wide awake through the passion of love. My heart
watches when love of you there grows more robust.
'I sleep and my heart watches.' I sleep for my friend
gives rest; I watch for he grants rapture. In the sweet
sleep of my repose, my anxiety to watch you becomes
a more watchful dream. Sweet the sleep and sweet the
dream: to know nothing else, to know you alone; to
have time for you and to behold you, so far as this is
granted here as if in a dream and in shadow and in
riddle.*

Of good vintage is the largess of this leisure and
vision. This vision has some likeness to a dream,
inasmuch as it occurs not through human choice and
effort, not through our investigation, but through
the visit of One rising from on high.* Paul sleeps, as it
were, when he dies to the world; he watches, as it
were, when he lives to Christ.* May my soul,
brethren, sleep his sleep and may my watches be such
as his. May they be continuous and uninterrupted.

Ps 75:7

Is 50:2

Qo 4:11

1 Co 13:12

Lk 1:78

*Rm 14:8; Ga 2:20;
Ph 1:21*

But now in a reversal I keep watch and my heart
sleeps; the spirit sleeps and the flesh keeps watch;
and if the flesh sleeps, still the spirit does not
immediately keep watch. Repose is granted to the
spirit, but the spirit is not yet absorbed and enrap-
tured by that intoxication of glory. It is asleep to
provocations but not yet aroused by invitations to
inebriation, but however frequently these may be
tasted, they still rouse the soul they inebriate with a
vital renewal.

3. Rightly are they called watchmen, who never
abandoned that inebriateng wine, who are always
aglow with the bounty of eternal delight.* Of such
watchmen you read in the book of Daniel.* Truly
they are sentinels in whom nothing needs to be lulled
to sleep but everything keeps watch for God. Truly
they are sentinels whose vigils are not interrupted.
They experience no feeling of the animal soul
which ought to be drugged that the watches of the
heart may be more alert. Some watches are filled with
the disturbing anxieties of which Peter speaks: 'Be
sober and watch, for your adversary the devil goes
about like a roaring lion seeking whom he may
devour.'*5 Paul also says: 'Watch and stand firm in
the faith.'* But not more free from anxiety are those
watches in which the doctors of the Church are
harassed, like the shepherds in the Gospel who
watched and kept night vigils over their flock.* Such
watches are disturbed by anxiety to ward off the
threat of evil.

The watches of the sleeping bride involve no precaution against evil but a profusion of good. Indeed
passionate love from yearning unfulfilled compels the
relaxed mind to keep watch. Something like a vigil is
desire for his coveted presence or delight in his
presence granted. A good vigil is devotion not drowsy
but alert, whether in access to the Beloved's presence
or in yearning for him in his absence. Devotion is
neither vigilant nor vigorous, unless the mind be
restless, but asleep to the concern and desires of the
world. Hence the bride says: 'I sleep and my heart
watches.' And in Job one reads that 'In a vision by

1 S 1:14
Dn 4:10

1 P 5:8
1 Co 16:13

Lk 2:8

night, when sleep overcomes men and they slumber in
their beds, then God opens their ears',* then he
speaks, then he knocks.

4. So this verse follows: 'The voice of my
Beloved as he knocks: Open to me!' Rightly she
keeps vigil, not knowing at what hour her Beloved is
to come. The vigils of the bride and the voice of the
Beloved apparently overlap. 'My heart watches,' she
says, and at once adds: 'The voice of my Beloved as
he knocks: Open to me.' My heart watches and my
Beloved does not sleep. His voice knocks and says:
'Open to me'. My heart watches and at once he comes
flying and his voice is heard: 'The voice of my
Beloved,' she says. This voice is known to me, this is
pleasing to me. To other voices I am deaf, to this
I am alert. As soon as it rang in my ears, I leapt for
joy.* Many voices are wont to make a din and to
whisper hollow flatteries, but not as the voice of
my Beloved.

Great is the prudence of the bride, brethren, and
endowed with discernment of spirits, for she knows
so well how to distinguish between the wiles of
demons and the true wooing of her Beloved. 'The
voice of my Beloved as he knocks,' she says. Whose
voice has the quality to match the voice of Jesus?
That of philosophers? Or of heretics? Or of the
Law? Or of the Prophets? His voice is vigorous, it
'has made foolish the wisdom of this world'.* The
Law and the Prophets led no one to perfection,* but
the voice of Jesus comprehends a summary of the
peak of perfection; his voice includes the precepts of
consummate perfection;* his voice moves the affections. 'The voice of my Beloved as he knocks,' she
says. For his voice knocks and penetrates as effec-
tively as a two-edged sword.* Gently it slips in and
courteously persuades as no other teaching could do.
Its language is not lofty but lofty are its mysteries.
Humility of conscience, harmony of morals, accep-
tance of obedience, purity of the flesh, contempt for
the world, desire for things eternal, knowledge of the
Godhead: what disputation ever delivered so much
in words or what strict observance was ever so

Job 33:15-16

Lk 1:44

1 Co 1:20
Heb 7:19

Si 43:29

Heb 4:12

inspiringly persuasive? Thanks to its teaching, we
have learned to hope and to sigh for the grace of
resurrection, impassibility in the risen body, eternity
of life, and the revelation of Majesty.

Ps 75:2 'God is known in Judaea; in Israel his name is
great.'* Was his name so great? Was it as well
expressed? Was it so published? Was it so broad-
cast? 'In Israel his name is great', but not as great
either in unmistakable teaching or in passionate devotion or in the countless hosts of believers. 'Of old
God spoke to our fathers through the Prophets, but
in these last days he has spoken to us through his
Heb 1:2 Son.'* Therefore it is a vigorous voice, a voice of
power, the voice of the Beloved; but it could not prevail in the ears of the Jews. The Gentiles heard and
confessed and did not contradict but said: 'The voice
of the Beloved as he knocks'. I recognize that both
belong to the Beloved: the voice and the knock, the
word and the power. With both, my Beloved is pleasing to me; with both, he charms and moves me, with
his voice and with his knock and, so to put it, with
canticle and with psalm.

Truly does he knock and, as it were, play the timbrel, for he inspires a harmonious symphony of word
and deed. Think of Jesus as a timbrel: approach,
touch, shake, replay his behavior, his deeds, his
words, his life. In him all the strings of the timbrel
are attuned and sonorous; when touched they ring
out a sweet melody. Jesus himself is both the
player and the instrument he plays. 'No one,' he
says 'takes my life from me but I lay it down and I
take it up again. I have power to lay it down and I
Jn 10:17-18 have power to take it up again.'* Consider what a
song he sings for you in his laying down and taking
up and in his power over both; consider what is the
reason for such music. Does his voice not play
especially upon our heart and waken our heartstrings,
that attuned like a cithera we may strive to harmonize
with him who rings out such melodies?[6]

5. 'The voice of my beloved as he knocks.'
Aptly does she say 'my Beloved', like one who calls
and knocks from sheer love and grace. 'Open to me,

for my head is moist with dew and my locks with drops of night.' Charity begins to grow cold in Judaea; already the trek towards the Gentiles is being planned according to Scripture.* To Judaea the word of salvation was sent, but she rejected the word, judging herself 'unworthy of eternal life'.* I have been locked out by her; do you open to me, 'for my head is moist with dew and my locks with drops of the night'. The head of Christ is God. The Jews take pride in God the Father; they boast that they have knowledge of him. His Son they reject and blaspheme; do you open to me. 'My head is moist with dew.' Those who reject him, his head does not long for, does not thirst for, but rather ignores; therefore his head is full of dew. It is moist with dew because they are fickle in understanding, lacking in depth of reason, devoid of conviction in their claims; trivial in reason, ponderous in obstinacy, ineffectual but tenacious like dew and drops of the night. 'And my locks' are filled 'with drops of the night' which are icy and dark. For there is a dew which does not belong to the night. 'Your dew,' says Isaiah to God, 'is a dew of light'.* 'And my locks' are filled 'with drops of the night'. The Jews have clung to figures, well versed in the literal but not in the spiritual sense.[7] The Jews glory in the knowledge of the One God and in figurative observance of the Law; discoloring the mystery of the Trinity and the truth of what was prefigured, they boast of superfluous and lifeless symbols. They annoy me, they oppress my disciples, who are like an ornament and decoration of my head; so I fly from them 'Open to me!'

6. Some heretics try to extinguish the light of Christ's divinity, which they refuse to approach by faith and cannot approach by reason. With the shrewd refinements of their disputations, as incoherent and minute as dew drops, they discolor, corrupt and suppress the subtle and converging written evidence which rests on divine authority like locks of hair on the head. These also, assuming a personal knowledge of God and an acuteness in spiritual discernment, as if loftily posted[8] on the very head

Ac 13:46

Ac 13:19

Is 26:19

and locks of God, are compared to the dew and drops of the night, that you may understand that they are tiny, frosty, fluid and incoherent.

If, however, you see someone clinging to a sound faith as if to the head itself, sharing in the sacraments only for appearances and skilled in shrewd inter-pretation, still his faith is frigid, thanks to a bad conscience, dark in its duplicity and watery thanks to its rapid evanescence. For 'the exultation of a hypo-crite lasts but a moment'.* Such a one Jesus considers an outsider, shuns as an oppressor and a burden to Himself. Such men do not so much walk as flutter upon 'marvels and wonders' beyond themselves,* in exalted pride hovering in a basket of air.[9] In their circuitous 'profiteering, they stalk in the dark'.* They hunt for gain from religion; they pretend to possess spiritual doctrine and an eloquence as fluent as dew; they claim to know doubtful, occult and, as it were, nocturnal mysteries, to grasp the head and summit of the wisdom of God's holiness and to cling to the very crest of Christ; they show determination to reach the pinnacle but not to enter the door.

Jb 20:5

Ps 130:1

Ps 90:6

7. In his annoyance Jesus shuns them saying: 'open to me, my sister.' Since you are within and do not wander abroad, or flutter aloft, or wish so much to be conspicuous outside as to dwell inside, open to me. 'Open to me; open to me.' What do you seek but me? You are wholly mine, wholly mine, and mine on many counts. How many? Listen to how many: 'My sister, my kin, my dove, my spotless one.' 'My sister' because related in the flesh he assumed. 'My kin' be-cause from his side while he slept on the cross, from the second Adam, the new Eve was created, that they might be no longer two but one flesh.* There is a natural kinship; here a personal union. There a sister; here a bride. 'My dove' by the grace of the Spirit; 'my spotless one' by forgiveness and discipline. In the flesh a 'sister', in the sacraments a 'bride', in the Spirit simple, 'spotless' in holiness, in all of these 'mine'.

Gn 2:24; Ep 5:31. See Lam. 6, n. 9.

'Open to me!' Do what you are doing; open to me! For you I am within but open to me in those whom

I still wait outside. Open, invite, and draw them 'into the site of the marvellous tabernacle'.* Knock, that to you may be opened 'a wide and inviting door', as Paul says,* that through your persuasions an entrance may open into their affections. Enter among them, that afterwards you may draw them to yourself. Go out to them that they may come in to you, for they shiver outside feeling the chill. Recoup the losses of your absence by gaining the presence of others.

Ps 41:5

1 Co 16:9

What do you say? 'I have put off my tunic; how can I don it again?' What do you say? 'I have washed my feet; how shall I soil them again'?* You have put off your tunic, the tunic of fleshly care, a tunic certainly cumbersome and perhaps soiled. You have put off your own tunic; don mine. Zeal for my house has consumed you; therefore, as Isaiah says, don the mantle of zeal.* Press on, prove, preach, beseech, in season and out of season!† To walk in this path is not to defile your feet.** If any dust clings, brush it off your feet.* Feet not defiled but fair Isaiah praises with the words: 'How fair upon the mountains are the feet of those who herald peace, proclaim good tidings.'* Do not delay, let the example of my deeds prompt you. My hand may touch you, if you hesitate at my word. 'I am a zealot';* do you also be zealous for me. Postpone your pleasant leisure; for a moment be involved in my business. Everyone enlisted in God's army must be involved in God's business when he hears the command.* Although I was rich, I became poor for all;* equal to God I emptied myself embracing the form of a slave.* For all I died, that they who live should no longer live for themselves but for me.*

Sg 5:3

Ps 68:10, Jo 2:17,
Is 59:17
†2 Tm 4:2
**Is 35:8
Mt 10:14

Is 52:7

Ex 20:5

2 Tm 2:4
2 Co 8:9
Ph 2:7

Rm 14:7-8

8. Heeding such examples in her Beloved and moved by them to emulation, the bride says: 'My Beloved thrust his hand through the latch-hole and at his touch my heart was thrilled.'* Through the narrow aperture of poverty, persecution and death, he inserted for me the examples of his deeds. These touch me; these move me. For the thrill of the heart means a stirring of the mind. Hear then the outcome of her emotion, for she continues: 'I arose to open to

Sg 5:4

Sg 5:5   my Beloved.'* Listen and understand, all you who quite precipitately and too shamelessly hasten to ecclesiastical preferment. For the bride to whom the love songs of this Canticle are sung approaches slowly and hesitantly, even after she has heard herself called sister, kin, dove, and spotless. Consider whether these qualities exist in you, and if they do, fear lest you lose them; if they do not, fear even more lest you fail to acquire them. Observe after how many invitations and eulogies she says: 'I arose to open to my Beloved.' Let it be futile for you to arise before you are summoned, for you are eating the bread and drinking the wine of that holy delight mentioned above: 'Eat, my friends, and drink and be

Sg 5:1   inebriated, most dearly loved.'* Let it be futile, nay frightening, for you to arise uninvited, when you are sleeping a sweet sleep until the Beloved says to you, 'Open to me'. Let not the voice of ambition, or avarice, or restlessness, or elation move or allure your spirit with deceptive flattery. Let those voices be unknown to you; let them not persuade you that the task is good for you, but arise only at the voice of your Beloved who lives and reigns God for ever and ever. Amen.

NOTES ON SERMON FORTY-TWO

1.   G. uses an intricate alternation of singulars and plurals of address, as if the one soul and the many souls were the one bride, the one Church: in par. 1, *vides . . . videte*; in par. 2, *fratres* but in par. 3, *legis*; in par. 4, *fratres* but *puta*, etc. . . . *Vide*; in par. 8, *audi . . . audite . . . attende* and a series of singulars where the individual soul and the bride seem to be fused together.

2.   Reading *invitationem* with mss and Mab. for *vitationem* of Migne.

3.   Reading *in commune* with mss and Migne for *in Ecclesia* of Mab.

4.   *diffinis* with mss, Mab. and Migne; see the same word in S 47:6.

5.   This verse is read daily at Compline. See Morson, 154; White, 7-11.

6.   See Hamlet's use of the same idea to disconcert Guildenstern who cannot play on the recorder or pipes and would play upon Hamlet. 'Will you play upon this pipe?' [the recorder]. When Guildenstern confesses that he cannot, Hamlet continues: 'Why, look you now, how unworthy a thing you make of me! You would play upon me; you would seem to know my stops; you would pluck out the heart of my mystery; you would sound me from my lowest note to the top of my compass; and there is much music, excellent voice, in this little organ; yet cannot you make it speak. 'Sblood, do you think that I am easier to be played on than a pipe? Call me what instrument you will, though you can fret me you cannot play upon me.' Shakespeare, *Hamlet,* 3:2. See John Hollander, *The Untuning of the Sky,* Princeton U. Press, 1961, pp. 206, 266, 270; he quotes Chrysostom who uses similar instruments to make the same point. See Gn 31:27, Jb 21:12.

7.   De Lubac, *Exégèse,* 2:291, n. 7.

8.   Reading *locati* with mss Paris 9605, Troyes 419, for *locatis* of mss Paris 8546, Bruges 49, Madrid 512, Mab. and Migne.

9.   This is reminiscent of Aristophanes' *Clouds,* where Socrates is satirized as a Sophist; he appears in a basket treading the upper air, in the clouds where thinking is clearer. Vainly Socrates attempts to counter the humor of Aristophanes in his Apology: Plato, *Apology,* 18, 19.

SERMON 43
FROM ACTION TO CONTEMPLATION

Receiving his inspiration for action, the lover is led to contemplation. 1. Yesterday we saw him seek solace, today see him bring solace. 2. The bride is invited to a higher contemplation. 3. The graces and actions of God vary with the variety of attributes; his simplicity receives various titles. 4. The meaning of the head and the locks bedewed with moisture; one must guard against the deceitfulness of Satan. 5. The bride makes excuses to avoid the care of souls. 6. The anticipatory grace of God and a triple manner of contemplation. 7. The three actions of the bride, thrilled, rising, opening. 8. Regular observance is compared to dripping myrrh and to the persecutions of the Church. 9. Action precedes contemplation.

OPEN TO ME, MY SISTER, MY KIN, MY DOVE, MY PERFECT ONE, FOR MY HEAD IS MOIST WITH DEW, MY LOCKS WITH DROPS OF THE NIGHT. I HAVE SHED MY ROBE. HOW SHALL I DON IT AGAIN? I HAVE BATHED MY FEET, HOW SHALL I SOIL THEM AGAIN? MY BELOVED THRUST HIS HAND THROUGH THE LATCH-HOLE AND AT HIS TOUCH MY HEART THRILLED WITHIN ME. I AROSE TO OPEN TO MY BELOVED, BUT MY BELOVED HAD TURNED AWAY AND GONE. MY HANDS DRIPPED WITH MYRRH AND MY FINGERS WERE FILLED WITH CHOICEST MYRRH.*[1]

Sg 5:2-6

515

I n the previous sermon our explanation of this passage suggested that Jesus begged for comfort from his bride against the assaults of those who try to stain the purity of our faith with the dregs of human and perfidious teaching, to drench it with the night dew of shrewd plausibility which the Prince of darkness, the Prince of the night air sprinkles covertly and imperceptibly.* Again in another passage, Jeremiah laments that waters engulfed his head.* In yesterday's talk then, the Lord Jesus was presented in flight from assaults; today let him be presented returning with joys. Yesterday he was presented as begging solace, today as bringing solace with him, yesterday full of insults, today full of graces.

Eph 2:2; 6:12

Lm 3:54

Yesterday's interpretation concerns but few souls; today's concerns many more. Not all are either suitable or commissioned for the work of preaching. For not all are equipped to refute attacks on the faith or charged with this task. Not all can be mothers and brides but all can be sisters and brides. Not all can sustain the pangs of childbirth but all must sustain the grace of his embrace. In yesterday's interpretation the moisture of the night dew was disagreeable; today let it be pleasant. There Jesus speaks to register complaints, here to suggest endearments. There he hid from his foes but here he only hastens to his bride.

2. 'Open to me, my sister, my kin.' Observe the discipline of the guard here, where the door is not left without a sentry. Who will enter at will there, where Jesus does not enter without knocking and only when his voice has been heard and recognized? Happy I should be, if it can be said of my soul: this door is closed and no undisciplined feeling slips through by stealth or by chance! It opens only to the Prince, if I set a guard over my lips to open only to the Prince when he halts before them. Open to me the gateway of justice* and entering through it I shall feast with you, I shall dine in justice* and shall drink and be inebriated; in the words of the Song, I shall also inebriate you with my dewdrops.* I come not parched but moist with the dew of graces flowing

Ps 117:19

Eph 5:9; Ph 1:11; Mt 5:6

Sg 5:1

gently. 'Open to me!' I am already inside for you now but open to me that I may enter more fully.

'Open to me!' I come at last renewed and with the dew of fresh affection. Like the dew, my eloquence will flow over you, when I shall let settle upon you the mysteries of my Godhead. 'My head is moist with dew' and contemplation of the divine nature in me begets subtle and fruitful meanings. Why do you tarry over the mysteries of my humanity only? Why do you crouch so long only at my feet? Arise, ascend to my head, open to my head. Open to me in my head, 'because my head is moist with dew'. My humanity purchases grace; my Godhead bestows grace. My humanity petitions grace, my Godhead imparts grace. My humanity pours out blood; my Godhead pours in love. 'My head is moist with dew.' My Godhead is really the dew. My Godhead seeps into the soul and waters her marrow. Up to a point I have entered, open to me, that I may reach your inmost being, that the sweet experience of my Godhead may pour in and dye every cell of your interior. Open to me that the fine dew of my Godhead may saturate and inebriate the soil of your heart.[2]

Yes, brethren, this is the real truth. Where there is greater glory in the subject matter, there is greater grace in meditation. What has more excellence, claims more reverence and confers more grace. What takes priority by the superiority of its nature, when it is grasped elicits more delight. That is more pleasant to all, which surpasses all. A special kind of vision is required for a unique object. This special vision is not within human rights, for it is not a human characteristic. This is granted to a restful and watchful mind, yet not when man wills but when God wills and says: 'Open to me!' What is it to say: 'Open to me', but with an endearing word to woo the affection and court the desire, that the mind touched in part by the flash of so much light may offer itself purified for a fuller perception? So the light, as it were, says to the eye, 'Open to me', and from a tiny glimpse of itself, light engenders a yearning for a greater participation.

3. 'Open to me, my sister.' Why do you request, good Jesus, that the door be opened? You yourself 'have the key of David'; you open and no one closes.* Your sudden appearance is an opening. Appear and no one closes to you. When the glory of your Majesty in its tiniest ray begins to flash upon the spirit, suddenly it whirls and sweeps the spirit towards itself. While your glory radiates, it allows no door to be shut upon it. The heart you penetrate, you open to yourself; you hold it open, as long as you do not withdraw yourself. And perhaps both openings are required and related, the opening of the Bridegroom and the opening of the bride. The opening of the Bridegroom is his appearance; the opening of the bride is her preparation and adaptation for such tender exchanges. 'My head is moist with dew and my locks with drops of the night.' His head is moist and therefore those who cling to his head are refreshed with its dew. Delightful is God in himself; delightful is God in his saints,* who rise from him through grace and by his design like distinct strands of hair cling to his head. Beautiful is the contemplation of God both in his essence and in the graces which proceed from him.

Indeed 'there are varieties of graces' like a distinction of locks.* For 'his invisible attributes'† seem to display some distinctions but only according to our limited capacity. For what in God is but one, becomes known as many and varied to us, as we strive to convey this or that divine attribute in distinct symbols and words. Some concern only his Magnitude; regard this as one lock of hair. Others concern his Power alone; so regard this also as one lock. Similarly what relates to his Wisdom, Goodness, Predestination, Providence, Grace, Clemency, Counsel, and in general our thoughts about God which one form of expression encompasses and which seem to belong to one attribute, interpret as one lock; those which relate to some other attribute, interpret as another lock.

'His invisible attributes', says the apostle, 'are understood when seen through his visible creation;

Rv 5:7

*Ws 16:20,
Ps 67:36*

**1 Co 12:4
†Rm 1:20*

so also his eternal Godhead.'* Paul speaks of these
attributes in the plural, of his Godhead in the singular. The Godhead then take as the head, the attributes
as his locks. For the Godhead in itself is one and
simple, but so far as it affects its subjects and
impresses its image on them individually, the Godhead receives many titles of different meaning. Thus
titles which denote God's essence can be predicted of
one another, but not titles which denote God's
attributes. God's essence is his knowledge, for these
are convertible in reality and in each his substance is
identical. Although it is true that God knows some
object, still it does not follow as a consequence that
he is that object. Likewise in God, Power is essentially
one and the same as Will. But the attributes ascribed
to each do not mutually follow each other. For
these attributes, since they involve some effect
related to creatures, draw from creatures a related
multiplicity and therefore cannot consort together.
A marvellous identity and a marvellous diversity!
Each is beyond explanation; each is full of wonder;
each contains most hidden and most effective mo-
tives for devotion and reverence!

4. Approach this head, O bride, and these locks
of your Beloved; comb out his 'locks moist with
dew'; thence you will draw a store of sweetest perfume. His locks are full of drops of the night, hidden
drops, drops refreshing with a sweetness not unknown. The time will come when such drops,
pressed out more often, will produce the force of a
full stream. Good is the stream which cools the
yearning of fervent love. Whether you understand
the head and the locks in the way explained above,
or take the head to denote that unveiled knowledge
of the Godhead face to face and the locks that
knowledge derived through a mirror and beneath
the veil of a riddle,* in each you will find abundant
dew for refreshment. The reason why dew is assigned
to the head without qualification, while the drops are
ascribed to the locks with the added phrase 'of the
night', is perhaps that 'this vision through a mirror
and in riddles' has some likeness to darkness, since it

Rm 1:20

1 Co 13:12

is less bright and less warm.

O holy soul, emulate the Bridegroom! Let your head and your locks become moist with the dew of devotion; your head with the dew of your intention, your locks with the dewdrops of your thoughts. Like drenched locks, let your thoughts be straightforward, combed out, rich, refined by the discipline of continence, drawn out by perseverance in stability, rich in exultation of spirit. Let them not be dyed in the least by the dark and cold dew of malice and wickedness, which the Prince of this night air* sprinkles imperceptibly and covertly. Beware of his deceitful dyes! Falsely he claims possession of that heavenly dew of your Bridegroom. Slam the door on him, and if he should say, 'Open to me, my sister,' disclaim any kinship with him. Any kin of his is not spotless. Perverted is his kinship, for contagion follows it. When Christ calls someone 'sister', he adds 'spotless'. Yield only when you can reply: 'The voice of my Beloved as he knocks.' The enemy acts timidly at his first approach. Like a spy who fears discovery, he taps, he does not knock. Your Beloved, wishing to be recognized, knocks loudly. 'Open to me,' he says, 'because my head is moist with dew and my locks with drops of the night', as if to say: Open to me, because I slip in, filled with the dew of grace. Open to me. Make yourself ready for so great a presence.

Eph 2:2

5. Then she replies: 'I have shed my robe. How shall I put in on? I have bathed my feet, how shall I soil them again'? You say: 'Open to me'. Behold, I have opened, I am ready, but I am loath to be disturbed again by household chores. I do not want to don my robe again, once I have shed it. How shall I don it? How? In no way! I do not agree. I cannot hear without annoyance talk of donning my robe again. I have shed a robe of wool and am clothed in finer material. I know how onerous is Martha's role, in what a burdensome robe she is clothed, how, busy with continual serving, she must keep soiled the feet of her affections and the steps of her tasks.

I cannot degenerate from a Mary to a Martha.

I have chosen the best role, to make my heart open and ready for the arrival of my Beloved. In Martha's role one does not seem to have suffered any harm; once relieved she hastens to return to Mary's role. Stripped of all worldly substance and without the deterrent of a veil, ready to contemplate the glory of the Beloved with a face unadorned and, as it were, unveiled, I will arise to open to him. This way is a beautiful way; neither can a soiled foot proceed along it, nor can a foot be soiled upon it.*   *Is 35:8* the way, for the Beloved stands at the door clamoring and knocking, as if chafing at delay. He knocks at the gate, he scouts the entrance and with more ardent love, despite my haste, he anticipates me.

6. 'He thrust his hand through the latch-hole and at his touch my heart thrilled within me.' What does it mean here that the bride who had closed the door of her room³ did not also block this aperture lest anything approach her unobserved? Acting rather cautiously in everything else, why did she allow a place for negligence here? Or was she less aware perhaps of this aperture in herself? Who indeed can know all the apertures, all the entrances, all the breaches⁴ in himself but the one who as we read in Ezechiel, bored holes in precious stones?*   *Ez 28:13* holes where he wills because where he wills through the latch, through an apt entrance, he thrusts his hand, the power of hidden inspiration. 'Through the latch-hole,' she says, that is through a suitable, a hidden, a narrow entrance. The entrance is narrow enough, where Jesus thrusts only his hand, in comparison with the opening of the door which he seeks. The bride's heart would not be thrilled, she would not rise, would not open to her Beloved, unless previously he had thrust in the hidden hand of his inspiration. Hidden is the cause of the first call, concealed its reason and not yet wide open is the entrance. But the entrance is widened when the soul cooperates with the Bridegroom who predisposes, and so makes an effort, arises and opens.

The first cause is recognized as the hand of God alone; the second as that of God and man together.

And while it belongs more to God as a gift, it is
ascribed to man alone as a merit. The knowledge of
God is also narrow and, as it were, conceived through
a latch-hole, knowledge derived from contemplation
of his works, as if it were the touch of his hand, not
the sight of his face. Notice a threefold manner of
contemplating: in the head, in the locks, and in the
hand: in the head the divine nature; in the locks, the
human form; in the hand, his handicraft. Of this last
we read: 'You have delighted me Lord, in your
handicraft and in the works of your hands I shall
exult.'* We can also name them as follows: essence,
signs, works. Signs through some likeness in their
genus promote a knowledge of the divine nature
which his works confirm. Signs, so to speak, illustrate
and works demonstrate. This last manner of contemplation belongs to simple folk, the second to the
learned, the first to those most purified. However, as
we said already, the insertion of his hand through the
latch-hole signifies that concealed and hidden impart-
ing of inspiration which the touch of divine power
effects.

    7.   Here also one can distinguish three actions of
the bride. What are they? First she is thrilled,
secondly she rises, thirdly she opens. The first
occurs in her but not at her initiative; the two following so occur in her that they are indeed at her initiative. In the first she is anticipated, in the second she
makes an effort, in the third she reaches her goal.
When she is thrilled she is not active but passive; when
she rises and opens she makes some effort on her
own. She is thrilled, when she gently experiences the
hidden movement of holy inspiration; she rises, when
she consents and follows where inspiration leads; she
opens, when her mind yields wholly to this work and
makes itself energetic. The more she opens herself to
this exercise, however, the more quickly she faints
through excessive affection and passion. 'I was mind-
ful of God,' says the Psalmist, 'and I was delighted
and exercised, and my spirit fainted.'* Compare and
apply memory to her heart, delight to her thrill,
exercise to her rising. For the words 'my spirit

Ps 91:5

Ps 76:4

fainted' refer to what follows in our text: 'I opened
the bolt of my door to my Beloved but he had
turned away.' He then turns away, when you faint,
unable to endure. When you are moved too passionately then he flies off more quickly. The more
affectionately you receive the embraces of the
Beloved and strive with an open heart wholly to ab-
sorb and consume him, so much the more quickly
the fleeting presence of your Beloved fades away.

8. But now let us return to the sequence of the
text. "I arose to open to my Beloved. My hands
dripped with myrrh; my fingers were filled with
choicest myrrh.' About to speak of opening the door,
why does she first advert to her hands? Did she wish
perhaps to suggest with what hands you should open
to your Beloved, with what meritorious deeds you
should prepare your approach to the contemplation
of truth? Good indeed are hands scented with myrrh,
which practice mortification of the flesh, which
check its laxity, constrain its wantonness, that the
entrance may be wider for enjoyment of the Word.
Do you not regard as drops of myrrh these works of
regular observance, which following one upon another anoint the mind and constrain the flesh? Consider our vigils, fasts, a modest and sparce diet, rough
cloth and black bread, strokes of the rod freely
undertaken, the chanting of psalms at daybreak[5] and
silent prayer; though each prayer rises with heartfelt
passion, still silent prayer is the more passionate the
more a quiet breathing of the body releases the
breath of the spirit. Do not all these observances
distill myrrh upon us as they succeed one another?
Rightly are they compared to myrrh, because they
inflict on the flesh the bitterness of discomfort and
soothe the spirit with the ointment of devotion.

That neither discretion is lacking in the bride nor
reasonable service,* you can gather from her words:
'My fingers were filled with choicest myrrh.' Deeds
are her hands; discretion her fingers. Myrrh is not
only the action of the flesh but also the anointed
exultation of the heart. This is choice myrrh,
although there is a myrrh which is counterfeit. When

1 Co 12:10;
Heb 5:14; Rm
12:1. See Lam
195, n. 164.

you see the fingers of some childish men casually
dropping forbidden signs, their dexterous hands
promiscuously scattering tokens of a wanton and
perverse disposition, in my opinion you will not
deny that they are pouring out like counterfeit[6]
myrrh the bitterness of an undisciplined life. Is not
such wantonness like myrrh, which both perturbs
the disciplined conduct of the brethren and will
beget for the offender in the future the grief of confusion and repentance?[7]

But that myrrh is the choicest which has been
found praiseworthy in the many trials of regular observance. Both regular observance and enemy assaults
are praiseworthy when the virtue of patience, re-
maining intact, is not destroyed or soured by excessive bitterness. Recall the times when the Church,
still a young maiden, beat upon the ears of the Gentiles, that she might open a door and clear an
entrance into their hearts for her Beloved, Christ.
What countless agonies of blood and tears she endured! How many martyrdoms she suffered! With
what continuous torments was she racked! Truly her
'fingers were full of the choicest myrrh', because in
her travails her virtue was chastened by the trials of
every form of suffering.

9.   With such hands, brethren, struggle to be open
to the Word, to build an entrance for the sweetness of
contemplation. By the merits of good deeds you will
more successfully unlatch for Christ the storeroom of
your mind. Consider whether the myrrh of your toil
and weariness in many trials has been found praiseworthy, as gold is tested by fire.* 'My fingers,' says
the bride, 'are filled with choicest myrrh.' The
nicety of discretion and the fruitfulness of anointing
are meant here, for she mentions her fingers and
fingers which are filled. They distill but are filled;
they experience loss and gain, but not bankruptcy.
Fasts alternate with repasts, labors with repose, vigils
with sleep. Alternation brings refreshment, not faint-
ness. 'My fingers are filled with choicest myrrh.'

Do you desire the delights of contemplation, to
enjoy at ease the embraces of the Bridegroom, to

*Ws 3:6. See Miquel
158, n. 30.*

clasp him alone in the secret of your heart? Do not
run to open [the door] with empty hands, with dry
hands! Action precedes contemplation.[8] The more
you mortify your animal impulses with the myrrh of
continence and penance, the more splendid the
entrance you prepare for your Beloved. In fact the
bride continues: 'I opened the bolt of my door to my
Beloved.' Within the narrow passage of our sermon's
ending we cannot open the door of this verse. Let us
postpone its treatment for another sermon,[9] as we
seek and await grace from him 'who possesses the key
of David', without which no one opens,* Jesus Christ   *Rv 3:7*
who lives and reigns for ever and ever. Amen.

NOTES ON SERMON FORTY-THREE

1.   G. writes for one individual but plurals are inserted for example in par. 2, *Et revera sic est, fratres,* and par. 9, . . . *fratres . . . Videte.*

2.   Reading *tui* with mss and Mab. for *tuis* of Migne.

3.   Reading *cubiculi* with mss Paris 9605, 8546, Madrid 512 for *cubilis* of mss Bruges 49, Troyes 419.

4.   Reading *aptitudines* of mss, Mab. and Migne, though one is tempted to amend to *apertiones,* which occurs in this paragraph or to *aperturas* of Am 9:11, *aperturas murorum.*

5.   *in maturinis.* See Jean-Marie Déchanet, 'La Contemplation au XIIe Siècle', in DSp 2:1950; Lam 170, n. 6; 174, n. 23; 187, n. 113.

6.   Reading *improbabilem* with mss, for *reprobam* of Mab. and Migne.

7.   Reading *in posterum* with mss and Migne, for *posterum* of Mab. See Robert Barakat, *Cistercian Sign Language,* CS 11 (1975). Lam 176, n. 39 and 173 n. 18.

8.   Leclercq, 'Otia Monastica', 105:15.

9.   *in alium differamus tractatum.*

SERMON 44
GONE FROM THE CLOISTER

The bride opens a cloistered door but finds him gone. 1. The door of our heart should be opened to God alone. 2. Three doors lead to God. 3. Frustrated longings increase the love of God. 4. The fervor and liquefaction of the soul in contemplation. 5. Climactic order is seen when the bride is thrilled, distills myrrh, and is melted. 6. Harshness towards penitents contradicts the example of the bride. 7. Melting of the heart increases humility and obedience.

I OPENED THE BOLT OF MY DOOR TO MY BELOVED. BUT HE HAD TURNED AWAY AND GONE. MY SOUL MELTED WHEN HE SPOKE*[1]   *Sg 5:6*

Today we shall discuss with you, brethren, the opening of the door. Now yesterday's sermon devoted the last paragraph of our treatise to the preparation which is, as it were, a road to the opening. Good surely is that preparation which always envisions the hope and beauty of immortality and incorruptibility, which does not sow in the flesh, lest it should reap from it corruption.*   *Ga 6:8* is always myrrh in my hands! 'If anyone,' says Jesus, 'does the will of my Father, he will know about my teaching.'* See how an act of piety gives access to   *Jn 7:17* truth. Good certainly are acts characterized by restraint and moderation and filled with the devotion of anointing. Rightly does one open to Christ with

527

hands anointed, for he received his name from anointing. And perhaps he knows how to enter only through a door anointed. Hence in the temple the little doors were made of olive wood, through which a way opened into the Holy of Holies.* For oil, also a product of such wood, is the handmaid of the fluid for anointing.

1 K 6:31

'Little' were the doors called and 'narrow' the entrance of olive wood; but sleek with the oil of grace you will slip through without trouble to where understanding is subtle and mystery hidden. An entrance will open without labor, if one wishes to use a door the oil of devotion and charity. I also think Paul's testimony concerning the temple is in agreement: 'For God's temple is holy and that temple you are.'* Have doors then in your temple through which the High Priest alone may enter the inmost recess of your heart. Shut the door, fasten the bolt, except when your Beloved knocks in his desire to enter. If no door exists, the entrance will be open indiscriminately to every itinerant. If the door is shut but not bolted, it will yield and open to a slight push, for it lacks a firmer enclosure! Have both the door of vigilance and the bolt of constancy. Look out vigilantly and resist constantly. Let no forgetfulness and ignorance infiltrate; let no wickedness burst in.

1 Co 3:17

Or, if you prefer the following distinction, regard careful forethought as the door and prayer as the bolt. Secured with such a barrier, your door will not lie open to hostile attack. 'He has strengthened,' says the psalmist, 'the bars of your gates.'* Do you not seem to hear 'bolt' and 'door' in these bars and gates? Each is necessary, but against the wiles of the enemy. When you hear the voice and knock of your Beloved, when you feel the delicate touch of his hand even through the latch-hole, slip back the bolt, open the door, let all barriers fall; if possible, remove the entire intervening wall, that your Beloved may pour himself into you freely. Let anxiety over the provocations of demons be turned into security in the presence of the Bridegroom; turn your precaution for repelling the enemy into full enjoyment of your

*Ps 147:13. See
Lam 185, n. 95.*

Beloved. The psalmist knew he had opened the door, when he said: 'My heart is ready, O God, my heart is ready.'*

Ps 107:2

2. Why does Jesus need a door? He says in the Gospel, 'I am the door'!* Here is a surprising paradox. He is the door and he knocks at the door. He wishes to enter, but through him 'whoever enters will be saved and find pasture'.* There is a great difference between one door and another. For there is a door of one kind in the evidence of nature; there is another door in the sacraments of the Church; there is a third door in the experiences of grace. At the first door, by the guidance of natural reason, wisdom acting through its works makes itself known to us; we gain access to some share of truth; we gather some knowledge of the Godhead, not however of the distinction of Persons in the Godhead. At this door the distinction of Persons is not made nor is grace conferred. Therefore at this door one should not delay forever or knock too long.* Through the second door, by our initiation into the saving sacraments, we enter the unity of the Church and the Communion of Saints. At this second door some so stand inside as to be half outside, until they approach the third door, which we interpret as a familiar access through the affection of charity to some enjoyment and contemplation of the Beloved. This door, so secret, so intimate, does not lie open to all but is reserved for the bride alone. In Ezechiel you read of many distinct doors,* but to visit them now would require a long digression. However, it makes little difference, I suppose, whether you visit him or he visits you, except that you then seem to visit him, when you take the first step and are the first to call upon him. But he visits you, when he takes the lead, knocks at your affections, slips in unexpected, and, when you have no such visit in mind, moves you with a touch of delicacy beyond your hopes.

Jn 10:7

Jn 10:9. See Lam 8 and n. 20; 10 and note 30.

Ws 13:1-9; Rm 1:20. See Miquel, 'Experience', 151-2.

Ezk 40 & 41

3. When he knocks in this way at your door, do not delay. Arise, hasten, lest perhaps he turn away. For this happens even in our verse: 'I opened the bolt of my door to my Beloved, but he had turned away

and gone.' Why go off, good Jesus? Why turn away?
Why cheat the beloved of her desire? Do you prompt
her desire and withdraw her delight? Or perhaps, in
this way, do you draw out her yearnings to greater
keenness and warmer desire by withdrawing your
presence? It is so. Obviously it is so. All the dis-
appointments of love add more fuel to love itself, and
all the deceptive wiles raise love to its peak.

Those appearances after the Lord's Resurrection,
how brief they were! how sudden! how interrupted!
By some he was at long last barely recognized and in
a flash he was gone. By others he does not allow
himself to be touched. For others he slips in through
closed doors, not requiring the opening of a door.
That door is indeed opened to him most of all which
is closed to all other commerce. When one supposes
him a captive, he spirits away his agreeable presence,
come like a thief, gone like a thief. The joy of contemplation is indeed like a momentary flash. Swiftly
it departs and in excellence it surpasses all the power
of human capacity. Whither it goes, in our human
flesh we cannot follow with matching strides. 'I said
I shall become wise,' Solomon recalled, 'and wisdom
withdrew further from me, much further than it was

Qo 7:24-25   before.'*

Perception of Wisdom teaches better than its
deprivation, how transcendent is its Majesty.[2] The
more passionate it is, the more swiftly it passes. 'He
had turned away and gone,' says the bride. *Did you
turn to the bride, good Jesus, precisely that you
might so swiftly turn away from her?* 'He had turned
away and gone,' she says. What does 'he had gone'
mean? He had gone beyond me, gone beyond my
powers, gone through me. So he went through me, as
one without strength to contain him and stand fast. A

Eph 6:17   sword is the word of God;* a sword is Jesus; he
passes through the soul without delay or difficulty.
The soul faints, when the mind dissolving cannot
sustain his passion. Fiery is this sword. Hence 'as

Ps 67:3   wax melts before the face of fire',* so the soul
enkindled melts before his face. 'My soul was melted,'
says the bride, 'when my Beloved spoke.' You see

how he melted her soul by his flaming word.

4. 'I opened the bolt of my door to my Beloved but he had turned away and gone.' So at the epiphany of the Lord's Resurrection to the two disciples on the way to Emmaus, when their eyes were opened to recognize Jesus, at the very moment of their opening, he vanished from their eyes and, as it were, went through their hearts, as they confess: 'Were not our hearts burning within us, while he was speaking...?'[3] Their hearts were burning within them during their colloquy, but when he manifested himself, their hearts melted, losing their firmness and consistency in that passionate vision. For what else does Jesus' disappearance mean but that they were unable to stand fast in the glory of his epiphany? He turns aside to his beloved like a river of peace, but like a torrent of glory he passes through. Like a fiery torrent he makes the soul melt which he floods, refreshes, and passes through. How sweet is the hour, when the soul, melting, merges with this fiery torrent![4] How refined is the soul at that moment, how delicate, how agile! Then it has no lukewarm drop, no filings of flint, no degree of frost! The soul is a fire and a flood!

Interrelated are flood and fire. In these two elements consists the practice of contemplation. What is liquid absorbs heat more readily, and vice versa the heat absorbed makes still more fluid the liquid it finds. What I call 'hot' and 'liquid' is what may be called by other names, 'inflamed' and 'unalloyed'. Hot it is, because it loves; unalloyed and liquid it is, because it mirrors in itself some likeness of the Beloved. Hot it is, because it yearns; liquid it is, because it beholds. Hot it is, because it is inflamed; liquid, because it is informed with the image of the Beloved.

What is liquid has nothing impure, nothing sluggish; it easily discerns and easily follows. But not so much grace belongs to liquid in the absence of heat. Well is that called liquid, which not only shares the brightness from the purity of the Beloved, but also, as if heated, bubbling, and boiling over, hastens after the Beloved who has already passed through it. 'He had already turned away,' she said, 'and gone' from me; he had passed through my whole being. Swift was his passing but with no little passion in his touch. After him he left my soul melted, poured out more abundantly and striving to pass over even to the passover to my Beloved, in no way counting on the return of his presence. At the voice of exultation I was melted in a flash when he spoke. 'My soul was melted,' she says. What does 'melted' mean? She began to expand, to run, to reflect; to expand beyond herself, to run towards him, to reflect him; to expand in virtue, to run in desires, to reflect from truth; that is, she became great-hearted, graceful, and glorious!

5. From this melting, perhaps it was granted to her that her hands drip with myrrh and her mind be melted. Why do we omit the third boon which the Canticle includes? Yes, it gives the following orderly sequence: 'My heart thrills, my hands drip, my soul was melted.' Even a cursory reader of this passage can notice a climactic order; yet it is not simple and easy to assign a reason for the gradual distinction. In all three, some measure is noticeable, but greater in the second than in the first and greater in the third than in the second. For it is more to distill than to be thrilled, as it is more to melt than to distill. The presence of the Bridegroom bestows all three on the bride; that her heart is thrilled, that her hands distill, that her soul is melted. All is from the touch of his hand and the sound of his voice; all is from his touch and so to speak, from his passing through. Because he touches, she is thrilled; she distills myrrh, because he seizes her and passes through her with a passionate spirit,* 'for its voice you hear but whence it comes and whither it goes, you do not know'.* Therefore her soul was melted as he spoke.

Ac 2:2
Jo 3:8

The voice is more subtle than the hand; it moves move passionately and it passes more swiftly. A sermon of Jesus is freighted with more subtle and more sublime teaching than any illustrations of his works can produce. His teaching on the majesty of the Godhead which he circulated among his disciples, surpasses every illustration; his promise surpasses all our experience of the future glory which will be revealed to us.* If you open the door of your mind to understand and perceive it, that you may comprehend this promise of glory, it immediately turns aside and passes away; so you should also pass into the affection of a melted heart. To this voice of the Beloved say: 'Wonderful, far beyond me is your knowledge, soaring far beyond my reach!'* Yes, my soul is melted, it falls short of comprehension and thanks to your passionately violent sweetness, is unable to stand and linger in wonder. For these and similar reasons the bride says: 'My soul was melted when my Beloved spoke.'

6. In your opinion—if I may introduce a digression and an added topic to exhort you—in your opinion, why does the Lord's discourse not cleave, like an icepick, the hardness of some people? Their bowels are frozen with chilling feelings of exaggerated austerity; their bowels distill no drops of mercy; they are not thrilled and moved with the slightest affection towards penitents. Why do they not feel the touch of his merciful hand? Why do they not become inflamed by colloquy with Jesus most solicitous? Why do they not hear Jesus knocking outside in the person of their penitent? I fear lest he turn aside and pass them by, that when they seek they may not find him, that when they cry he may not listen. Why are your bowels hardened towards your sons, as if they were not yours? You could perhaps have looked upon your own sons with a merciless eye and passed them by in unheeding contempt, if they were yours only and not also your Lord's. How hard you would become, if you were obliged to give alms from your own possessions, when you dole out even to your sons the Lord's possessions with so niggardly and grudging a disposition?

'He distributed liberally,' says the psalmist, 'he gave to the poor.'* Perhaps you do not know the poor. What if God should say to you: did your eyes not see my imperfect one? In your book are only the

Rm 8:18. See Miquel, 'Expérience', 153, n. 10.

Ps 138:6

Ps 111:9

Ps 118:16

perfect inscribed?* Was no anxiety for those on the
road to perfection ever wont to detain you? He is a
bad physician, who does not need the sick but perhaps gives ulcers to the healthy![5] If you are unwilling
to seek the prodigal, at least meet him on his return.
Open the gate of mercy and if you will not lift up the
penitent for Christ's sake, at least lift up Christ in the
penitent. Let your soul melt with the dew of mercy
and be set on fire at the cry of Jesus as·he calls
and knocks.

The voice of the penitent, the voice of the poor, is
the voice of Jesus. Therefore when you hear this
voice, let your soul melt in feelings of compassion,
that you also may be able to say with the bride: 'My
soul was melted when my Beloved spoke.' Listen and
recall his word to Mary Magdalen,* his word to the
woman taken in adultery,* his word to the Samaritan
woman,* his word to the Canaanite woman,† his
word to Zacchaeus,** his word to Peter,†† his word
to the centurion.* After so many words of pardon
and mercy, whose feelings would not be softened,
whose bowels would not melt? After so many passionate gusts from the south, even from the hardest
breast, the frost of no matter how many years could
be melted. I feel that I am drenched through in a stream
of overflowing oil and that I am melting with similar
affection, as often as I recall the works, the words, the
precepts of your mercy. 'This word of yours burns
passionately and your servant loves it dearly.'* He
loves because he needs it; therefore my soul loves and
melts for joy when you speak.

7. Every holy man must feel this melting. For the
melting we discussed above belongs only to the perfect and is theirs, not always, but only in due season.
Yet, not to withhold in fruitless silence what occurs
to my mind, I shall give you briefly the rest of my
thoughts about this melting. Do you not see how
what is melted begins to be moved from its stiffness
and immobility, how it strives to go out from and
abandon itself, how from its original swollen mass, it
flows downward, descends and vanishes, how easily
following its guide even to lower ground or, searching

Lk 7:38-50

Jo 8:3-12

*Jo 4:7-42
†Mt 15:21-28
**Lk 19:2-10
††Mt 26:75
*Mt 8:5-10. See
Lam 7, n. 15.

Ps 118:140

for lower ground of its own accord, it often runs ahead of the effort of its guide? In those so melted, great is the readiness and prompt the will to follow their guide.

You understand at last, I imagine, in persons thus melted a growing aptitude for obedience, the docile affectivity of a humble soul. This humility fear does not deform but the warmth of charity informs. Fear breaks the mind with violence; love softens it and, by making it pliable and liquid, fashions it at will. Humility issuing from charity suffers no uneasiness, of its own accord seeks the lowest level, and rests when it has reached the lower vallies. At last in 'melting' you have in a concise expression, the nature of a noble humility, you have the nature of obedience. Would you also like the scriptural evidence? 'The Lord opened my ear' that I might listen to him as a master.* You have heard him speak as Lord, now hear his melting affectivity as a disciple: 'I offered no resistence,' he says, 'I did not turn my back.'* You hear how he is a follower; now hear to what depths. 'I gave my back to the strikers and my cheeks to those who plucked my beard; I did not turn my face from those who reproached me and spat upon me.'* Does your Lord not step down to the rough and lowly road, not stubbornly resisting but melted and docile on hearing the fiery word?

So one who melts with the affectivity of such humility and obedience and is not frozen stiff as a swollen block of ice, in his own right gloriously adopts the words of the bride: 'My soul was melted when my Beloved spoke.' O wonderful power of the word so passionately burning! It sets the heart on fire, converts the loins, reduces the soul to nothing in its own sight in comparison with God,* makes the soul melt and run from self, so that the soul is no longer with self but as the psalmist continues: 'I am always with You'.* Therefore the soul is neither in herself nor with herself but with her God: ever attentive and as far as allowed ever following, but not always reaching her goal either to her heart's content or in that eminent way proper to a bride with

Is 50:5

Is 50:5

Is 50:6

Ps 72:21

Ps 72:23

her Bridegroom. For even here the bride continues:
'I sought him and did not find him; I called him but
he gave me no answer.'* But this verse calls for discussion at leisure and must be kept for another time.
What we have said will be enough to match not the
magnificence of the subject but our limited power to
suggest how the soul of the bride melts at the call
of her Beloved, Jesus Christ, who lives and reigns for
ever and ever. Amen.

Sg 5:6

NOTES ON SERMON FORTY-FOUR

1.   G. addresses one individual, except in the first sentence of par. 1, the last sentence of par. 3, the first sentence of par. 6, and in par. 7.

2.   Reading with mss, Mab. and Migne: *Perceptio ejus melius quam privatio docet quam sit transcendens ejus majestas,* although Mabillon's suggested interchange of *perceptio* and *privatio* is attractive.

3.   Lk 24:13-32, expressed in Migne, omitted by Mab.

4.   Cf. S 16:9; See M.-André Fracheboud, 'Divinisation: IV. Moyen Age. A. Auteurs Monastiques du 12e Siècle. 2. Cisterciens', DSp 3 (1957) 1407.

5.   *Malus medicus qui non est opus aegrotis, sed bene habentes fortasse exulcerans.* Mt 9:12.

SERMON 45
HER MANTLE FROM THE WATCHMEN

At the advice of the watchmen the bride dons or discards her mantle. 1. Why this alternation in the presence and the absence of the Beloved? 2. The watchmen are the holy doctors through their writings. 3. A preacher's rebuke should be taken in good part. 4. Good and prudent masters speak for our benefit. 5. Various cloaks are better removed. 6. Such a cloak is the heavy mantle of office. 7. This we should be happy to have removed by the city watchmen. 8. Some are too attached to this mantle of office.

I SOUGHT HIM BUT FOUND HIM NOT; I CALLED HIM BUT HE GAVE ME NO ANSWER. THE CITY WATCHMEN FOUND ME, THEY STRUCK ME AND WOUNDED ME. THEY TOOK AWAY MY MANTLE, THEY WHO GUARD THE RAMPARTS*[1]   *Sg 5:6-8*

When your Beloved has left you, he does not return to you when you will. This distress gives understanding to love and an increase of affections. Now he visits his beloved; now as her visitor vanishes, he distresses her. Alternately he ravishes the heart's desire of a lover and then restores it for love's engagement. When the Beloved has spoken, your soul melts. Your soul in melting faints, unable to endure, and your Beloved turns away. Your fainting prompts his flight. When your Beloved is present and speaks, you melt, faint and swoon; in his absence you are allowed a breathing space. In his absence he restores the forces which his presence exhausts. Intervals cool the passion of delights, for you could not endure this passion were it continuous. Why do I say 'continuous'? Does not its very beginning leave you exhausted? For as soon as the Beloved speaks your soul melts.

Later in the Canticle the Bridegroom says: 'Your eyes have put me to flight.'* How have they put your Beloved to flight except by fainting from excessive affection for him? You know no moderation; therefore your Beloved is moderate and allots for you in due time the measure of his presence. So you seek but do not find; you call but he gives no answer. Observe, brethren, the passion and the power of love. It neither suffers the absence of the Beloved nor suffices to sustain his presence. In his absence, love's longings, labor for breath; in his presence, love's longings, surfeited, suffer a relapse. O happy love, which with endless ebb and flow either melts in him or, in seeking, sighs for him. 'I sought him but found him not,' she says. 'I called him but he gave me no answer.' Elsewhere this is expressed as follows: The wicked will seek and not find me; 'they will call but I shall not answer'.* Why is the same clamor and pursuit so common to good and to wicked men? *Why, good Jesus, do you withdraw indiscriminately from both? No, not indiscriminately, but with much discernment.* Of the wicked it is said: 'They shall seek and not find.' Yet the bride does not despair of finding him but complains of not having found him. 'I sought him but found him not; I called him but he gave me no answer.'

2. O how often I have sought the Lord Jesus in meditation, invoked him in prayer! But neither did meditation grow sweet nor prayer affectionate. So I 'found him not' and he 'gave me no answer'. I found him not in person; no, nor his gifts, but sweet beyond measure are the answers he gave. O that he would answer me often when I read or pray! *Yes, good Jesus, tell me 'the number of my iniquities and sins; show me my crimes and omissions'. Hide your face for a while,* that my foulness may become known*

Sg 6:4

Ho 5:6, Pr 1:28

Jb 13:22-24.
See Lam 178-9,
nn. 49-52;
185, n. 95.

*to me for my salvation, either in my meditation or in
my reading of sacred Scriptures.* Then indeed the city
watchmen, the holy doctors, discover me when I find
my conduct in their writings. Then they discover me
when they paint my character and vices; they strike
me with their lightning strokes, they wound me with
thunderous denunciation.

The sacred writers like watchmen of the holy city
Jerusalem, which is the Church, search out the various
affections of spirits and discover the passions and the
good qualities of each and the disease under which
each labors; no one's thought escapes their search. As
often as I read their works, I think I am discovered
and caught. They pierce and wound me with the
javelins of their exhortations, while they convince
me that what I thought hale and hearty is bleeding to
death. They remove the veil of pretence, the shroud
of ignorance or forgetfulness, the cloak of false glory.
They strip me of the wrappings of hypocrisy and the
trappings of pride as if of a mantle. They strip me of
the mantle of glory deceitfully donned, as they lay
bare the weaknesses of my conscience. Profitably
then, in this way I am discovered by the watchmen,
although I cannot discover my Beloved at will. Like
Paul, finding less reason to take pride in myself, less
reason for complacency. I begin to burn with brands
of love for my Beloved.[2]

3. 'Daughters of Jerusalem, . . . tell my Beloved
that I languish with love.' On my own I dare not
approach him; I do not claim for myself such
familiarity. Jesus does not yet grant me access to
himself. Therefore, daughters of Jerusalem, I approach you, I solicit your help, I put my case in your
hands. I charge you with my business: 'tell my
Beloved'. As if he does not know, dissembling all
the while! Let the watchmen plunder, let the daughters tell, let the doctors exhort, let the daughters
implore! 'Daughters of Jerusalem, . . . tell my
Beloved that I languish with love.' Tell him, inform
him; your oft-repeated hint will sway my Beloved. I
am already unfrocked, I am already stripped of myself, I am fit now to be clothed with my Beloved. A

mind stripped and disengaged languishes with love.
'Tell my Beloved that I languish with love.'

Brethren, if a doctor's scathing rebuke seems to be
aimed at you in particular, to strike your conduct
expressly, to lay bare the wounds of your mind, to
strip off the cloak which conceals or blinds your conscience, make that a spur for your love and not fuel
for your hatred. Why does each of you construe as a
personal insult what is addressed to all in common?
Perhaps his discourse applies to you, yet it does not
mention you by name. Let the general reproof bring
you the languor of love, not the passion of complaint. And if you do not yet languish with longing
for that sweet love, it is well if in the meantime you
languish with shame for your fault, if you languish
with repentence, if your flesh is pierced by fear of the
judgement. Be converted in your grief, 'while the
barb is fixed' in you.*

*Ps 31:4.
Lam 193 n. 158*

Confess your fault and allow the cloak of concealment, with which by dissembling you hide your
acts of injustice, to be taken from you. Do not more
rigidly and more stubbornly cover yourself in the
cloak and wrap yourself in the shroud of hypocrisy.
Jesus will not be converted to you, unless the veil of
pretence and deceit has been taken from you, the
veil which shame and the fear of displeasing wove for
you. Shame has covered the face of your conscience;
remove the veil of shame, put on the veil of confession. For even the Lord puts on confession, not his
own but your confession. With this cloak he considers himself adorned; this he borrows from you.
Hand him your cloak, which he receives from you
with affection as a pledge of love and a sign of
reconciliation. Then you will begin to languish with
love, although previously you languished with feelings of repentance. Then the daughters of Jerusalem
will begin to commend you to your Beloved; then
heavenly spirits and spiritual souls sharing your joy
will proclaim that you languish with love.

4. But from an abundance of matter concerning
the state of repentance we are treating this passage,
though all its features seem to breathe out something

more perfect, more in harmony with that grace which deserves to be considered in the status of a bride. 'I sought him,' she says, 'but found him not; I called him but he gave me no answer. The city watchmen found me.' She seeks him by meditation; she calls him by prayer. By listening to teachers she is found, struck, wounded and robbed of her robe. And lest anything be wanting to her crown, she is helped by the commendation of the daughters of Jerusalem, that is, of faithful souls. Observe four points here, either in her or about her: search and longing, precepts and prayers: the searches of meditation, the longings of desire, the precepts of teachers and the prayers of the faithful.[3] Are not the precepts and exhortations of teachers often received with profit by those whom both anxious search and sincere prayer could weary? Are not indolent yearnings quite often aroused by stimulating words? In Acts what is fervent is made more fervent by these encouragements.*

Ac 18:25

'The city watchmen found me.' Good and prudent masters adopt a vagabond style, one reminiscent of the hunter's art, and adapt their discourse to various states of mind in the hope of finding someone they may touch, stimulate, move, someone among their hearers who may take pride in saying: 'The city watchmen found me, they struck me and wounded me.' The more perfect one is, the more easily he is wounded and tender affection feels more quickly the shafts of language. O happy the spirit, which such sublime darts of exhortation reach, which they find vulnerable to their wounds, for then these darts do not glance off, deflected by the hardness or obtuseness of their audience. Such darts are not to be flung at random nor in every crowd, but only where apt minds are believed to be found, which such excellent teaching will not elude. These barbs are like lightning; they strike the heights; they shun the plain; they discover the peaks; they strike the peaks.

5. So the bride says: 'The city watchmen found me, they struck me, they wounded me, they took away my cloak.' They took away the cloak in which as a penalty Adam was wrapped when stripped of the

splendor of his former simplicity. They took away
the coverlets of fantasies by which he was interiorly
impeded; they took away the cloak, the veil of symbols, and introduced the truth. The simple truth,
revealed and manifest, begets the fervor of love.
'Therefore, daughters of Jerusalem, tell the Beloved
that I languish with love.' However sincerely anyone
may think he enjoys the vision of understanding, as
long as the truth, though perceived, does not please,
does not ravish and inflame the affections, he endures the veil, the covering of bleary eyes, the cloak
of concealment. But when this veil has been taken
away, then truth dawns, it sparkles and kindles love.
Then anyone enduring this passion will be able to invite others to share his rejoicing: 'Tell the Beloved
that I languish with love.'

Consider Judaea. As long as truth lay hidden beneath the covering of the Law, as long as she endured
the veil of blindness, languishing in fear and paralyzed in emotion, she could savor nothing sweet or be
wounded by no arrow of divine love. When, however,
turning to the Lord, she laid aside the veil, when this
cloak was taken away from her, then she began to
make her own the words of this glorious confession:
'Daughters of Jerusalem, tell the Beloved that I
languish with love.' Then, glorying in the taste of a
new and unwonted sweetness, she invites the daughters of Jerusalem to give thanks and by her example
allures her fellow kinsmen. In our Canticle listen
to their response, when they are challenged by such
an invitation: 'What is your Beloved like? We shall
also seek him with you.'* You see how they yearn to
become sharers in her faith and teaching. Teach us
'what your Beloved is like and we shall also seek him
with you'. Make us sharers in so great a grace,* that
in our zest for the search we may begin to languish
with the affection of love. Let these brief observa-
tions on the mystical meaning be sufficient.

6. Now let us return to what was the occasion for
our digression; we were explaining the advantage of
removing the cloak. The words which diverted us
were: 'They took away my cloak'. Let us probe this

Sg 5:9

2 P 1:4

passage a little longer; let us explain this cloak.
Indeed it is not the simple cloak in which even holy
minds are wrapped. It is a 'double-wrap', that is, a
cloak wrapped around twice, perhaps even three or
four times.* How many kinds of cloaks have we set   *Ba 5:2; Ps 108:29*
before you? Are not the care of souls and the
anxieties of temporal administration already a cloak
heavy and burdensome enough? Let me speak more
plainly of my own troubles. I know what it is to be
weighed down by this cloak, how arid the soil I was
allotted, how barren the fig tree. Many a year has
already slipped past, as I approach or rather stand
by, watching for fruit on my fig tree and finding
none. How often it has disappointed our hopes and
baffled our labor and thwarted our expectations?
With good reason do I call this cloak burdensome
and the less useful it is, the more burdensome it
becomes. For the burdens of office are lighter when
alleviated by the abundance of the harvests.

Woe to me that the city watchmen found me, that
they thought they found something in me deserving
of such a burden! They struck me, wounded me,
filched my cloak and after inflicting wounds de-
parted leaving me half dead.* They filched my   *Lk 10:30*
cloak, the cloak of simplicity, the cloak of light, the
amice of gladness, the vestment of burning affection.
How often was I wont to be wholly wrapped in such
cloaks, to be kept warm in saffron! But now the live-
long day in my mind I embrace and traffic in what
Paul called dung.* The comfortable cloaks I boasted   *Ph 3:8*
of, they took away and invested me in others that were
a burden. When will these be taken from me? When
shall I cast them off, if indeed I be allowed to cast
them off? Happy the day on which, divested and
relieved of this cloak, I shall invite you daughters of
Jerusalem, with more open-hearted affection to share
my joy! when you, who have experienced nothing
like the burden I now lament will feel gratitude for
the languor of love renewed in you! Pitiful indeed is
the man who, divested of such a cloak, grows pale
with grief and chagrin, instead of languishing with
love! A true bride, thus divested of the duty or

the practice of solicitude, does not languish with disgust but with the quest for love. Therefore she asks others to rejoice with her and to thank her Beloved.

7. When the primitive Church sought Christ in Judaea and suffered rejection, not finding a place for him among them, not finding Jesus there, she passed to the Gentiles. Among the Gentiles she sought him, called him, and among many 'she found him not', received no response but the response of death. Yes, initially, by the princes of this world as if by the city watchmen, how the martyrs were wounded, robbed of their goods, mangled in body, divested of the mantle of their own flesh! In so many and such vast rivers and whirlpools of tortures, charity was not extinguished in them but they languished the more in an increase of love. It seems pleasant indeed, since the opportunity arises from our text, to recall the unwearying charity of the martyrs amid so many kinds of torture and death, to recall how they assuaged their bodily affliction with the interior affliction of love. For if you apply this passage to them, theirs is not a cry of lament but of glory, when they say: 'The city watchmen struck me, they took away my cloak.'

Similarly we should not take it ill, if sometimes the watchmen on the ramparts divest us of the suffocating cloak either of troublesome care or of activity that is either not good or perilous. When Elijah was being carried off he threw away his cloak;* Joseph escaped though his cloak was caught;* the bride bore it well when her cloak was taken. Elijah cast off the veil of mirror and symbol, being swept away to see face to face. Joseph fled from the trappings of the world as if from great burdens, suspecting a source of temptation. Divested of anxiety, the bride is more free to capture the favor of her Beloved.

By the imagination, as if by a veil, the intellect is prevented from contemplating the real truth. Affection smothered in the cloak of honors and dignities is prevented from hastening freely to the things of God. Worrisome care overclouds, imagination obscures and honor assails all joy in the soul. In the first there is

2 K 2:13
Gn 39:12

deep shadow, in the second temptation, in the third
travail; in the first there is gloom, in the second
cupidity, in the third anxious care. 'The watchmen
on the ramparts took away my cloak.' Good are the
watchmen; they know well from whom they should
take the packsack of troubles, which soul they should
relieve of burdens and set free for the tryst with the
Beloved to seek and enjoy him. For frequently he
slips away and can be sought only with carefree affection. Good watchmen know then whom they should
spare from burdens and the straits and troubles
of activity, that they may hasten more freely to
meet and embrace the Word. They know whose cloak
they should take away by gentle persuasion. 'I have
taken off my robe', says the bride.*   *Sg 5:3.*
                                                        Lam 20. n. 85.
8. This indeed she said earlier but now she says:
'They took away my cloak.' She is revealed to herself
in pure and naked simplicity and with her affections
free for the engagements of love. 'They took away
my cloak', as if to ask her, 'why, bundled up in
anxieties, do you seek your Beloved? Why involve
yourself in these troubles? If you do not simply
relinquish your office, why do you not at least
relinquish your worries for a while? We do not withdraw you from your interests, but we wish you to
reduce their intensity. Do not allege necessity as a
pretext for excessive effort. Why allow the good
talent in you to be overwhelmed with earthly
cares? Why emulate those who, appointed to office,
are compared to beasts of burden? They gape open-
mouthed at the earth, their maw crops the earth.
With zest they ruminate upon it, they devour it with
relish and though they have a lofty position they
wallow in the mire.'

Do not emulate these passionate men. Be not
jealous of those who commit this iniquity.* Is it not   *Ps 36:1*
great injustice and inequity to train the mind to hit
ephemeral targets but to fall short of eternal targets?
What if their aim is not always ephemeral business?
What if some of them, on the pretext of providing for
necessities, excuse themselves from manual labor,
from meditation and from zeal in the search for

truth? What if they pay more attention to business than to repose, more to frivolous talk than to the weighing of sacred Scripture, more to idleness than to work?[4] They make the rounds of the workshops and cells of the brethren, idly, inquisitively, loquaciously.

Do not emulate such busybodies, such idlers. Convert all your leisure, both what you are offered and what you manage, to the commerce of love, to meditation on wisdom,[5] to zeal in quest of your Beloved or to his embrace after his discovery. By these and similar exhortations the watchmen on the ramparts took away my cloak. These are the watchmen of whom Isaiah says: 'Upon your walls Jerusalem, I have set watchmen; all day and all night they shall not be silent.'* But let us now fall silent here; let us be silent after this sermon, to pay our debts of prayer and praise, silent for the moment vocally but in spirit ever rendering the sacrifice of praise to the Lord Jesus, the heavenly King and Bridegroom for endless ages. Amen.[6]

Is 62:6

NOTES ON SERMON FORTY-FIVE

1. G. addresses one individual except in one sentence of par. 1, *fratres,* in one sentence of par. 3, *fratres;* in par. 8, he suggests his desire to resign or to be with his Beloved eternally. Mikkers, 39, suggests that par. 6 was addressed perhaps to nuns; but G. may be apostrophizing the 'daughters of Jerusalem', as in par. 3, which is addressed to *fratres,* and whom in par. 4, he interprets as 'faithful souls', *filiarum Jerusalem, fidelium scilicet animarum.* This is not to deny that at some time this sermon had been adapted for nuns; see 'Nuns in the Audience of Gilbert of Hoyland', 11 (1976 Kalamazoo Cistercian Studies Conference).

2. Rm 2:17-20, 2 Co 10:7-12:10, Jr 9:22-23; see David M. Stanley, *Boasting in the Lord: the Phenomenon of Prayer in St. Paul,* (New York: Paulist Press, 1973) 46-49.

3. Reading *sanctorum* with mss Paris 9605, Troyes 419, Mab. and Migne, though *sociorum* is found in Paris 8546, Bruges 49, Madrid 512. Lam 184-5, 89, 95.

4. Lam 21, n. 90 and 175, nn. 27, 30, 36.

5. Lam 183, nn. 78, 80.

6. Lam 173, n. 18.

SERMON 46
LANGUISHING WITH LOVE

*The bride languishes with love. 1. She relies on
the prayers of others. 2. Signs of love cannot be
hidden; a brother's virtues rather than his vices
should be heralded. 3. A hint of one's needs is
petition enough; what is the meaning of languor?
4. Passionate love brings languor of the flesh
and of the mind; love is more fervent in prayer.
5. Three kinds of languor and the languor
of love.*

I ADJURE YOU, DAUGHTERS OF JERUSALEM,
IF YOU FIND THE BELOVED, THAT YOU TELL
HIM I LANGUISH WITH LOVE*[1]

Sg 5:8

The order is appropriate. After the exhortations of the teachers, the bride seems to ask
from her companions the help of their prayers.
Her simple request is confirmed by an adjuration: 'I adjure you, daughters of Jerusalem, if you
find the Beloved, that you tell him I languish with
love.' Her adjuration shows the passion of her
prayer. Fretful desires cannot be content with their
own merits; therefore they beg help from the
prayers of others. Perfect humility always relies on
the merits of others. 'I adjure you, daughters of
Jerusalem,' she says, 'if you find the Beloved.' Hers is
not the hypothesis of a doubter, but the thoughtful-
ness of a petitioner, as though she said 'if you find
him' but meant 'when you find him'. I use the
conditional form, not in doubt of your finding him

but rather out of respect for your shyness. For you hear my request more calmly, with its indefinite condition rather than a precise time: 'When you find him'.

She is not afraid they will take her conditional request as an insult; she knows the shyness of the daughters of Jerusalem; she knows their humble spirit and that a precise definition would be more harmful to their tender modesty than a hesitant condition. 'If you find him,' she says. I say 'If you find him'; I do not say 'When you find him'. I say the one but I mean the other. This hesitation does not proceed from my affection but I suit my conduct to your feeling and to your most humble opinion of yourselves. 'If you find him', that is, 'when you find him', remember me when it is well with you. Then remember me, that you may hint, that you may carry the message to my Beloved. There is no need to delay in discussing this text. However, you might consider your own conduct, brethren.

2. Call to mind how you beg one another for the help of prayers, with what humble feelings, what earnest desires and what adjurations. Not that all of you would dare to ask us to communicate the news that you languish with love. Usually you lament in turn over the languor of one another; you do not glory over it. And if someone can glory for a moment, it is not prudent, lest perhaps your glory be brought to nothing by the intrusion of vainglory. Yet there are some who, by the witness of their life and the service of their lips, cannot hide the languor of divine love in themselves. The lips of a lover cannot fail sometimes to give birth to the desires conceived. For the spirit filling one's interior secretly draws forth a word for the consolation of others, pours out an abundance of infused grace. Even in this verse of the Canticle the bride does not speak; the Spirit speaks in her.

Aspirations in holy conferences, sighs emerging from the depths of the heart and frequent sobs, are these not emanations of the spirit and of grace conceived? Does the languor of love not betray itself

by such evidence? Languor is not hidden when sobs
are not concealed. Languor betrays itself when it produces such evidence. What results from witnessing
these signs? Do they not possess some power to evoke
wonder, so that they arouse emotions of thanksgiving
in those who are witnesses? Even if nothing be said,
the holiness of devout conduct amounts to a re-
quest.* Holiness wishes to be commended to God, *Lam 193, n. 150*
when it betrays itself by signs. What follows? When
I detect this heavenly love in someone, do I not consider myself in some way adjured to give heartfelt
thanks for him. Shall I not commend in devout
prayers the languor conceived, which a deep sigh
betrays? I am a hard man if I do not commend with
all the prayerful earnestness within my power so holy
and divine a passion in my brethren, if I do not commend it by supplication and repeat and announce it
to the Beloved, should the opportunity arise.* *Lam 18,*
nn. 76, 78.

But what is any one of you doing who prefers to
count the vices rather than the virtues of your
brethren, their losses rather than their gains, to condemn rather than to commend? If you do not feel
yourself sworn to recommend, you are no longer a
daughter of Jerusalem but a daughter of Babylon.
O wretched daughter of Babylon, who will repay
you in kind, as you repay? for repaid you shall
be!* Unlearn the ways of a daughter of Babylon. Put *Ps 136:8*
aside your savage ways. Cease to enumerate in the
saints their losses rather than their gains. Let your
malice in enumerating satisfy yourself alone. At least
do not herald the numbers abroad, do not proclaim
them to your companions. For companions of the
Bridegroom do not lend an ear, if you disparage
the bride. The Bridegroom himself is loath to hear
insults to his beloved. Whomsoever you inform you
inform him, 'for a jealous ear hears everything'.* It is *Ws 1:10*
rash to condemn the beloved to her Beloved.[2] He
prefers that good news be reported to him about his
bride and he lends an ear more readily to praise.

3. The bride knows this and so she says: 'I adjure
you daughters of Jerusalem, if you find the Beloved,
that you tell him I languish with love.' 'That you tell

him', she says. A report carries the weight of a
request.[3] Reflect on the way men usually make a
request. If you report someone's plight to a com-
passionate person, are you not making him a request?
A modest hint is an effective petition.[4] To point out
the infirmities of the distressed, the misfortune of his
lot, the arrogance of his foes, to whisper this in the
ear of someone in power, I say, what else is this but
to prompt his assistance by a respectful prayer? In
how many passages of the psalmist will you find this
form of prayer! In the Gospel Mary says to Jesus:

Jn 2:3. Lam 171,
n. 10.

'They have no wine.'* She does not petition her
Lord or command her Son, content merely to report
the lack of wine. That is the way to act with bene-
factors and with' persons inclined to liberality. For
a favor should not be extorted by pressure, but the
opportunity should be presented. Commend the bride
to the Bridegroom; enumerate her endowments. Is not
this to enkindle his desire, to apply the spur?

'Tell the Beloved.' To give the message is to challenge him to repay her in kind, to rekindle the em-
bers of one languishing with love. He has a store of
consolations in his heart but he waits to be prompted

Lam 190, n. 135.

by our prayers.* What he does he will do more
quickly if we knock, perhaps also more abundantly.
This delay means travail for me but it begets a
wealth of consolation. When prayers are multiplied
he will pour out more plentifully your long-awaited
consolations. 'Tell the Beloved I languish with love.'
You tell him, you who have familiar access to the
Beloved. Tell him, you daughters who have experienced how great for a lover is the power of weakness, how 'love is as strong as death', how 'jealousy is

Sg 8:6

as cruel as the grave'.* 'I adjure you that you tell the
Beloved I languish with love.' Tell him the news and
he will listen to your cry, to give warmth to my desires. 'Tell him I languish with love.' Love does not
languish but the lover languishes. Where love thrives,
there languor thrives, if the object of love be absent.
What is this languor but affection for the absent
Beloved consuming the lover?

4. Passionate love affects at once the flesh and

the mind of its patient. It extinguishes the wantonness of the body; it restrains the happiness of the mind. It extinguishes the movements of the flesh and restrains the cheerfulness of the mind by a feeling of sadness and a longing for the absent Beloved. The flesh languishes while its movement becomes more languid and slack. The spirit languishes while it is consumed by excess of ardent desire. Languor of the flesh is either the absence or feebleness of its motion. Languor of the soul is its excessive emotion. Is not the flesh consumed by the very fact that the mind, withdrawn from love of the flesh, is turned to other things? The movement of the flesh is not felt, while the spirit, become more passionate, can hardly be endured. Sometimes indeed it cannot endure, when too ardent a love exhausts the powers of the suffering spirit. For what is the strength of the human mind that it should endure, when that heavenly love of the Bridegroom drives it impatiently. Melted in this engagement, the spirit flees from itself, unable to bear the violence of love. Similarly, when fuel has been used up and at last burns low, the flames of a fire die down. Likewise, our God is a consuming fire.* He surely feels the force of this verse, who languishes with too passionate an affection, overjoyed and distraught and consumed in meditation upon his God.*

Dt 4:24

Lam 183, n. 81.

O powerful and overpowering passion of charity! If charity is not tempered, it cannot be tolerated. Rightly is charity powerful, since it makes the spirit it possesses powerless over itself. Once enkindled in the mind, charity reaches from end to end mightily.* It achieves its objective and prospers and grows and does not grow faint until it has made the soul faint. For just as the languor of our body is not always of equal violence but at times the body suffers more intensely, so also the affection of love, although it tends with continual desire towards the Beloved, sometimes burns with more intense yearning, especially at the hour of prayer. Then indeed the lover languishes, because a passionate spirit passes through him and does not remain. With the lapse of that hour

Ws 8:1

he can say: 'Daughters of Jerusalem, tell the Beloved that with love' I am melted and dissolve. Before this hour there is languor but at its end languor is turned to dissolution.

Therefore when you pray, do not allow your spirit to waver or to turn to other things, that touched by this happy passion your spirit may cling to it, becoming more fully imbued, penetrated and consumed. For this passion will not cease until it courses through and drains a person's whole spirit.* So Daniel, that man of desires, languished after this heavenly vision, so that no strength remained in him.* When that vehement passion has passed through, the bride returns to a more endurable and more human languor, which for her is continuous because it is not so aroused. Here, to be sure, even if she does not faint, she still grows pale with love for her absent Beloved. Good is her languor, by which the feeling of the flesh moves languidly. It is one thing if a carnal attack strongly mounted is checked by the arrival of a stronger force;* it is quite another thing, if languishing and, as it were, gasping its last, the flesh with a dying effort makes some feeble attack.

5. I still feel other irksome languors, all none the less useful: the languor of fear, the languor of weariness, the languor of sadness. Why should I not be consumed with fear and grief from awareness of a life spent worthlessly? with fear of an easy relapse in a life lived amid pitfalls? in a life passing in weariness, 'passing in a dream'?* Yes, 'every living man is nothing but vanity'.* *Would that some daughters of Jerusalem, O Lord, might tell you my languors if there be any in me worthy of your attention! For many languors in me require healing. How happy would I be, if some heavenly centurion were to say to you: 'Lord, my servant is lying paralyzed at home in terrible distress'! Please answer at once, Lord: 'I will come and heal him'! Say but the word, Lord, and I shall be healed. With a word you are present to help, since you are the Word. Great is the power of healing in the Word, both the Word which you are, O Lord, and the word*

Lam 192, n. 144.

Dn 10:8-10

Lk 11:22

Ps 38:7
Ps 38:6

which comes from you through those who are yours.
The centurion felt this, for he said: 'Lord, say but
the word and my servant will be healed'.* Mt 8:6-8

But hollow is all the talk of a teacher, O Lord, if
you do not speak within. Say but the word and my
languor will be healed; perhaps also a languor will be
begotten in me as you speak, that I also may dare to
say: 'Daughters of Jerusalem, tell the Beloved I
languish with love.' Both languors are good, the one
passionate and aroused and the other continuous and
moderate; except that the moderate is not really
continuous; because if often becomes the passionate,
breaking out and failing in self-control, thanks to the
unrestraint of ardent desire. It does not return to
itself, until it faints again. If you love for the moment
and afterwards cease, that is not love. If you love and
for love of the absent Beloved you do not grow pale,
that is not languor. Therefore that love may be
languor, let it have both qualities: continuity and
consuming power. 'Tell the Beloved', says the bride,
'I languish with love.' Those suffering from illness
want their illness revealed to the physician; those who
suffer from love wish it revealed to the Beloved, the
former to be healed but the latter to be renewed.
Emulate, brethren, this better languor, which as it is
created by the desire of the Beloved when he absents
himself, so is renewed by delight in the Lord Jesus
when he presents himself, the Bridegroom of the
Church and of a holy soul, who lives and reigns for
ever and ever. Amen.

NOTES ON SERMON FORTY-SIX

1.   G. writes for one individual, with plurals, *fratres,* in the last sentence of par. 1, the first of par. 2, the third of par. 3, and the last of par. 5.
2.   Reading *dilecto* with mss and Migne, for *delicto* of Mab.
3.   Reading *effectum* with mss and Migne, for *affectum* of Mab.
4.   Lam 188, n. 110. Reading *modesta suggestio* with mss Paris 9605, Bruges 49, Migne, although *modestia suggestio,* modesty is a hint, is striking, with mss Paris 8546, Madrid 512, Troyes 419 and Mab.

SERMON 47
THE BEAUTY OF THE NAZARITE

*His bride teaches others the glory of the
Nazarite. 1. The daughters of Jerusalem also
want to know what the Beloved is like.
2. Spiritual writing, so useful as medicine and
food, is rightly commissioned only of some
monks. 3. How the Church is beautiful, though
some members have stains. 4. How quality and
equality apply to the two natures of the
Beloved, so that we can say: 'like Father, like
Son', and 'like Mother, like son'. 5. In Father
and Son is a wonderful equality and a wonderful quality of likeness. 6. O bride, your faith
and love make you beautiful. 7. Our holy conference on divine subjects is admirable. 8. The
bright colors of the Nazarite and his bride have
faded from their pristine beauty in our Order.*

WHAT IS YOUR BELOVED LIKE, BORN OF
ONE BELOVED, O LOVELIEST OF WOMEN?
WHAT IS YOUR BELOVED LIKE, BORN OF ONE
BELOVED, THAT YOU THUS ADJURE US?*[1]   *Sg 5:9*

These questions so passionate seem to be
poured out with great feeling. From chats
with the languishing bride, I imagine, a similar
languor either newly created or awakened to
greater intensity, has emerged in the daughters of
Jerusalem. In a subsequent verse they even say:
'Where has your Beloved gone? We also shall seek
him with you!'* As if to say: we shall seek with you   *Sg 5:17*

but for our benefit also, desiring to enjoy him with you. In that text they do not say: we shall seek him for you, but 'we shall seek him with you', choosing for themselves also a share in her blissful discovery.

Great is the humility in both, in the bride and in the daughters of Jerusalem. She asks to be commended to the Bridegroom; they ask to be informed about the Bridegroom. Neither uses a simple request, but she asks with an adjuration and they ask with a repetition. Now the fact that she adjures and that they repeat their question indicates no trivial request. 'What is your Beloved like,' they say, 'born of one beloved, O loveliest of women? What is your Beloved like, born of one beloved, that you thus adjure us?' To good purpose were they adjured, seeing they are so inspired. Not slight is the value of a holy conference. Through the word the languor of charity is brought to birth and the languor of infirmity is healed. The centurion knows that the power to heal is effective in the word and therefore he pleads: 'Say but the word.'*

Mt 8:8. Lam 180, n. 65.

2. Good it is if words be spoken but it is not less good if words be written. 'For the word flies off beyond recall' unless it is bound fast in script.[2] Writing makes the word both durable and visible; entrusted to the page, it will be recalled when you wish. A book is a good trustee surrendering exactly what it received; whenever you wish you may select it; wherever you wish you may read it; as long as you wish you may dally with it. Writing is a mirror for the memory because it pictures the word. There in safety you store the medicines of the word, for there they are kept unharmed. If the word has the power to heal when it is spoken, why does it not have the same power when it is read? If healing is good when you speak, why is it not good when you read?

Your objection, 'Let not my languor be healed in this way!' can be paraphrased: 'let the man who first hears it enjoy the benefit of the word; let it not reach to later or to far distant generations. Where first it is spoken, there let it be stifled; let all its value be exhausted at its first hearing; let it be interred in everlasting silence. Let it not fall again on good ground to bear fruit. Let the poor fellow who first receives this medicine, recover from his illness; after him let no one feel its curative power.'

At that pool in the Gospel, one man used to be healed after the movement of the water, but in that one man was the symbol of charity, not of singularity.* After the cure of the first man in the water, *Jn 5:2-9* it was not said of that pool: 'empty it out, empty it out, right to the bottom; let no trace of the healing water remain'. A good movement of the water is the treatment and the rustling of the sacred page! For it is well moved when, after a prudent airing, one is advanced to spiritual understanding. It is well moved when by dispersing the words one auditor is lifted forward.

As the word is medicine, so also it is food. And how can you say: let the food you produce perish, let it not endure? Yet this permission to distribute food is not to be granted to all indiscriminately. The movement of the water healed only when the angel came down in his own time and moved it.* He is an *Jn 5:2-9* angel, to be sure, whose 'lips guard knowledge' and from whose mouth knowledge of the Law is to be sought.* Therefore, and this must be admitted, great *Ml 2:6* is the value in composing the word of salvation, but only when this task is entrusted to, or better, exacted of some individual. The caution then of our elders in imposing silence as a rule would seem to require no refutation; however ample their caution, it does no harm, for the permission profitably granted to some might prove the occasion of rash presumption for others, while a man might be engaged in a task not imposed on him to the neglect of the task imposed.[3]

3. Again, to return to the matter in hand,[4] much aroused and inspired were the daughters of Jerusalem by the conversation and adjuration of the bride. How would they not be inspired to ask about his beauty, when they see the bride languishing and almost lifeless for love of him? The languor of love detected in his bride, prompted their eagerness to seek him.[5] For seeing that the love in his bride was passionate,

they suppose that the causes and provocations of so much affection[6] are in the Bridegroom. They ask with affection what manner of beauty exists in the Bridegroom, for they cannot but assume that he is amazingly beautiful and they take the beauty of his bride as proof that the Bridegroom is most beautiful.

'What is your Beloved like, born of one beloved, O loveliest of women?' The loveliest of women is the Church, for she is the beauty of individual souls. She is most beautiful in whom all beauty exists and no blemish exists. Scripturally, as far as souls belong to the Church they are without blemish. If a blemish seems to exist in some souls, although an ugly stain spreads over some of her members for a time, the stain is not imputed to her provided it does not linger in her. Perhaps, once cleansed of the stain, her loveliness is greater than the ugliness she contacted from the sudden spread of the stain. Truly then she is 'the loveliest', possessed of all beauty and free of all ugliness.

But many faithful and spiritual souls are also most beautiful, either because by their holy way of life they allow no stain or by careful and sincere confession they at once wash any stain away.* Most beautiful in a way is one who, without surpassing all others, still does not transgress. There is, as it were, no transgression when there is a speedy recovery. Most beautiful then is the soul which dons splendor and confession,* clothed in light as in a robe.* Most beautiful is the soul which either is light itself or is clothed in light: by confession clothed in light, by its way of life existing as light itself.

4. 'What is your Beloved like, born of one Beloved, O loveliest of women? What is your Beloved like?' This repetition does not lack great affection nor does it lack a hidden meaning. But if the first question had been so phrased: 'what is your Beloved like, born as he is from a Mother beloved?' instead of 'from one Beloved', no one would doubt that the second question should be referred to his generation from his Father and the first to his generation from his Mother. For in each birth he is wonderful and

Lam 193, n. 158.

Ps 108:1

Ps 103:2; see Lam 6, n. 8.

exceedingly desirable but much more wonderful from his combination of births. Of his two natures, one he holds in common with his Father, the other with his Mother. This combination is proper to himself. What is personally his is considered to be shared with them, because he is integrally perfect from them. For he is constituted by two natures but none the less he is constituted in these two natures. He is constituted by them conjointly and he is constituted by each of them singly. From their combination and not from each taken singly is constituted the fulness of his personal prerogative, by which simultaneously he differs both from his Father and from his Mother. He differs from each of them and from anyone other than himself, not in one or other nature taken separately but in both taken together. What he is essentially by nature [human and divine] is constituted in some respect[7] by each nature taken separately and not by both natures taken together.

Simply and of himself he is God, as also is his Father; and simply and of himself he is man, as also is his Mother. He is not partially and only in some respect God, nor is he partially and only in some respect man. So in his entirety he is called God and in his entirety he is called man; his entirety means not the whole which belongs to him but the whole which he is; not as if in every part he were God and in every part man, but because he is not partially God and partially man. The fact then that he is called wholly God and wholly man, excludes rather than includes parts and posits essential simplicity in each nature, not because each nature is simple but because he simply is each of the two.

For that reason he is said to 'appear clothed in the likeness of man',* for although humanity is not connatural to divinity still humanity by being assumed in the person of Jesus, by clothing of a kind, dresses and covers his divinity. Human nature is not connatural to divine nature but we claim only that properties belonging to human nature exist naturally in the person of Jesus himself. Thus in his human nature Jesus is naturally man, true man, and truly man: true man thanks to the reality of his

Ph 2:7

human soul and of his human flesh; truly man because
truly constituted by his human soul and human flesh,
constituted by true human realities and truly constituted by them, not merely having true parts of
humanity and truly having them but also truly existing by virtue of them. Yes, having them as natural
parts and having them naturally, just as he is God by
nature so also he is man by nature and does not only
appear in the clothing of man. Rightly therefore, just
as Jesus is spoken of as existing in the reality of his
divine nature, so[8] he is believed to exist in the
reality of his human nature, having both natures and
having them naturally.   .

5. Therefore the daughters of Jerusalem, inquir-
ing what he is like according to each of two
generations, in their desire to be informed about his
nature ask two separate questions: 'What is your
Beloved like, born of one Beloved? What is your
Beloved like?' In his divine birth, he is Beloved and
born of one Beloved; in his human birth, he became
one beloved and was born of her who is beloved,
except that he is not so much Beloved because of his
Mother as she was made beloved because of him. All
that the Beloved has, he has from his Beloved
Father, but not all from his beloved Mother; rather
indeed all that she has she has from him. Therefore
when the daughters of Jerusalem ask the first
question: 'What is your Beloved like, born from one
Beloved?' they do not add a similar question: What
is your Beloved like, born from her who is beloved?
but simply 'What is your Beloved like?' Because in
the first question they express desires beyond the
powers of their understanding, they withdraw an
unlimited question and turn to a question more
human and more modest.

We can understand this however in either of two
senses, so that either the question is taken as repeated
on account of the twofold nature in Jesus, or[9] that
the first question because impossible to answer is
replaced by a second question, as if their question
'What is your Beloved like, born of one Beloved,
O loveliest of women?' were to mean: the truth

of this very faith[10] which you hold concerning the generation of the Beloved from his Father makes you the loveliest among all the followers of all the sects. Your faith purifies you, gives you charm, for by your faith you vindicate your Beloved as the equal of the Beloved from whom he proceeds.

He is of the same nature as the Father from whom he proceeds. A marvellous equality and a marvellous quality! That equality has the force of identity, that quality of the force of substantiality. If there were two natures each supreme, one in the Father, another in the Son, there would indeed be equality but there would not be identity. But the divine nature does not admit another nature equal to itself. In each the equality is one in number and is a substantial quality, indeed a quality that is substance. Therefore that the Son is such as the Father is means that the Son is identically what the Father is. Like Father, like Son! And the likeness itself is each one of the two, consubstantial with each, and it is one and the same substance with each one of the two. The substance not only confers subsistence but is itself subsistent, living, powerful and intelligent.

6. Such a one you proclaim your Beloved, born of a Father Beloved; such a one you define him. If it is possible, explain to us the reason for this faith and it is enough for us. 'Show us the Father, and it is enough for us.'* How shall we know what your Beloved is like, born from a Father Beloved, if you do not teach us what the Father is like from whom he proceeds? But this explanation belongs neither to the present time nor to our present capacity; it is enough however, to believe that the Son is such as the Father is. Although we are incapable of grasping what that likeness is, teach us what is his likeness according to our humanity in which he is the Beloved born of a Mother beloved.

Jo 14:8

Teach and tell 'what your Beloved is like'. It delights us to hear again what we have already heard about him. Repeat for us what either must be believed or can be grasped about your Beloved. To hear both fills us with passionate delight, and what

exceeds our capacity, captivates us none the less; we
have been captivated with your own fervor of wonder
and love, because we see you so captivated, so
arrested, so inflamed. O what is he like? O how
lovable is your Beloved? For love of him ever
increases in you, because to you he is ever the
Beloved born of the Beloved, indeed ever more
Beloved born of the most Beloved. Your love of him
makes you beautiful; your encounter with him makes
you desirous and your desire for him makes you
fretful. For it is thanks to your fretful and yearning
affection that you so adjure us. 'What is your Beloved
like, born from one Beloved, that you so adjure us?'
How beautiful is he, for he does not tolerate the
existence of anything ugly in you and therefore
made you the most beautiful of women! How lovable and gracious is he, for you cannot bear to be
without him even for an instant and for his sake you
so adjure us!

7. I ask you, daughters of Jerusalem, daughters
of this earthly Jerusalem, why you do not address
these repeated questions to the Church? Why do you
pretend not to learn of these two births in Christ, in
whom you refuse to believe? Why do you not consider yourselves adjured by the Church, when evidence
is brought before you based on faith in your own
Scriptures, on spiritual graces bestowed upon the
same faith, on martyrdom suffered for the same
faith? Why do you not consider yourselves, as it
were, adjured by the Church in the more appropriate
ceremonies she observes, in the more subtle tenets she
expounds, in the higher rewards she expects, in the
stricter vows by which she forms herself? Stricter
discipline, more integrated doctrine, a more simple
liturgy, and more eminent virtue could beget zeal in
each of you, challenge your affection and possess
the power of adjuration to arouse your emulation.

But a time will come, for it is not yet, when after
your conversion to the Lord the veil of ignorance and
pretence will be taken away. Then restored to your
senses, as it were, and receiving the Spirit of the Lord,
you will understand the power of these adjurations;

then awakened to a holy curiosity you will eagerly
repeat these questions, asking: 'What is your Beloved
like, born of one Beloved, O loveliest of women? What
is your Beloved like, that you have so adjured us?'
The hour of the Jews has not yet come, my brethren,
but ours is ever at hand. Therefore omitting frivolous
and deceitful talk, let us engage in the interchange
of such questions and expressions of wonder in our
communities.[11]

8. May you be the kind of daughters who long to
hear such truths! May I also be the kind of bride
from whom you may have the strength and readiness
to seek such truths! O truly blissful mother who
deserves to hear this apostrophe addressed to herself,
'Loveliest of women'. Blissful assuredly if she keeps
so much beauty unsullied. 'Her Nazarites were purer
than snow,' says Jeremiah, 'whiter than milk, more
ruddy than coral, more beautiful than sapphire. Now
their countenance is blacker than soot.'* Great cer-   *Lm 4:7-8*
tainty is this commendation but pitiful is this transformation! Purity of snow, whiteness of milk, red
glow of coral, brightness and beauty of sapphire are
overlaid with the blackness of soot. 'Now their
countenance is blacker than soot; they are not recognized in the squares.'* Indeed they are no longer   *Lm 4:8*
recognized as Nazarites in the squares.

I shall be silent about others. Behold the men of
our Order! How admired their name used to be over
the face of the earth!* In the beginning when they   *Ps 8:2*
were rarely seen in the squares they were at once
recognized for the sign of holiness in them. But now
they are distinguished and marked out from others
by little or no difference in religious observance, by
little or no distinction in their way of life. Therefore
they are not recognized as Nazarites in the squares.
To haunt the squares tarnishes the Nazarites' color
and gives them a foreign look. 'Their excellent color
has changed; the stones of the sanctuary have been
scattered at the head of all the squares.'* Therefore   *Lm 4:1. Lam*
'they are not recognized in the squares'. Not recog-   *195, n. 162.*
nized in them is their purity of birth, nor whiteness,
nor ruddiness, nor beauty. For whatever these colors

signify, they portray great beauty. Therefore 'they are not recognized in the streets'.

These are the colors of Nazarites; these are the colors of the bride and of the Bridegroom. For the bride also speaks in this passage and says: 'My Beloved is radiant and ruddy.' Such is our Nazarite to whom the colors of Nazarites are compared and also the colors of the bride. For she is a Nazarite, vowing and espousing herself to the Nazarite, Lord Jesus. Now when we discover her as a Nazarite, let us commend her beauty and consult her experience.[12] 'What is your Beloved like, born of one Beloved, O loveliest of women? What is your Beloved like, that you have so adjured us?' But at last let her compose the praises of her Beloved, the Lord Jesus who lives and reigns for ever and ever. Amen.

NOTES ON SERMON FORTY-SEVEN

1.   G. addresses one individual throughout, except *dicitis* in par. 2, *fratres mei*, in par. 7, and throughout par. 8.

2.   Horace, Ep. 1:18:71; see also his *Ars Poetica*, 390; see Lam 178, n. 48.

3.   RB 38:5. See Bouton, *Fiches Cisterciennes*, 150-51; J. M. Canivez, *Statuta Capitulorum Generalium Ordinis Cisterciensis* (Louvain: 1933-39) I:26 (Mikkers).

4.   Reading *revertamur* of mss and Migne, for *revertamus* of Mab.

5.   On *curiositas,* and *sancta curiositas* below, par. 7, see Lam 184, n. 92.

6.   Reading *affectus* of mss and Migne for *effectus* of Mab.

7.   *naturalis ejus essentialitas secundum quid.*

8.   Reading *sic* for *sed* with mss; Paris 9605 omits the line; Madrid 512, for *divinae* reads *dominicae* and concludes: *utrobique naturalia habens et naturaliter.*

9.   Reading: *Possumus autem utroque sensu haec* (mss Paris 9605, 8564, 473, 474, Bruges 49, Madrid 512, but *hoc* in Mab. and Migne) *intelligere, ut aut interrogatio propter geminam in Iesu naturam* accipiatur congeminata, aut (mss Paris 9604, 8546, 473, 474, Bruges 49, Madrid 512; for *dum* of ms Troyes 419, *cur* of Mab. and Migne) *illa prior quasi incapabilis hac sequenti sit revocata: Qualis est dilectus tuus, etc.*

10.   Reading *hujusce* for *Hujus te* and linking this with the preceding sentence, despite the mss, Mab. and Migne.

11.   Lam 175, n. 34, and 18, n. 75.

12.   Miquel 152, n. 5.

SERMON 48
RADIANT WITH LIGHT, RED WITH FIRE

The bride shows her Beloved radiant with light and red with fire. 1. His bride teaches her daughters about the Bridegroom; 2-3. that they also may be transparent with truth and aflame with love.

RADIANT   AND   RUDDY   IS   MY   BELOVED
DISTINGUISHED AMONG TEN THOUSAND*[1]   *Sg 5:10*

'Radiant and ruddy is my Beloved, distinguished among ten thousand.' The bride interrupts her quest for her Beloved for a time, but only a brief time, to instruct her daughters. She interrupts what is delightful for what is necessary, but not without love does she review in memory her eulogy of her Bridegroom. Sweet indeed to the lips of the bride are her praises of the Bridegroom. As a loving mother and a prudent bride she instructs her daughters and commends her Beloved. Rightly is she prudent, having topics so well prepared and abundant to discuss about the Bridegroom. Lovingly everything about him she has noted and pondered and it is on the tip of her tongue. Every detail elicits her affection for it is so firmly fixed in her memory. His color, head, hair, eyes, cheeks, lips, hands, body, legs, feet, throat, all these are described figuratively in her praise of the Bridegroom. And as if summarizing the whole description in a phrase and a brief heading she says: 'He is wholly desirable.' Then in order to show that in these words the nourishment of

her love is prepared, she says: 'Such is my Beloved
and he is my friend.'

In all this observe the teaching of the bride, observe
her devotion, observe her loving preparation, whether
seeking her Beloved or instructing her daughters or
recalling his praises. She adjures earnestly, she answers
readily, she illustrates with ornaments, she divides
distinctly, she reviews briefly, she sums up concisely
and I do not know whether she expresses sufficiently.
I know indeed that she concludes affectionately:
'Such is my Beloved and he is my friend.' Great is the
compass of these praises and obviously great is her
love when she praises.

2.   Let us now review the individual details of this
praise. 'Radiant and ruddy is my Beloved, distinguished among ten thousand.' This is a singular
blend of colors, which only in the person of the
Lord Jesus converged into one by the action of God,
not so as to be a unity but to be in unity. O gracious
and surpassingly lovable Bridegroom in whom the
divine generation is radiant and the human generation
is ruddy! For he is the radiance of eternal light;*
even if 'not born of blood nor of the will of the
flesh nor of man's will',* yet he is born of the blood
of a Mother. But there is in him nothing of that scarlet of which Isaiah speaks: 'If your sins were as red as
scarlet, they shall become like bleached wool.'*

The whiteness of wool and the blush of scarlet do
not blend together, do not tolerate each other. There
is indeed another redness which is found together
with radiance in the apparel of Jesus. 'Why,' says
Isaiah, 'is your apparel red?'* The apparel of the
Lord Jesus, his nature from virginal birth, radiant
with the purity and innocence of holiness, in the
affections of believers glows with a more comely
red from the color of his Passion freely embraced.
What is the quality of this red which lacks no longing
to cleanse all things? 'They have washed their robes,'
we read, 'and have bleached them in the blood of
the Lamb.'*

3.   This red in my Jesus discovers but did not
create this radiance; but his red makes, because it

Ws 7:26

Jn 1:12

Is 1:18

Is 63:2

Rv 7:14

does not discover, radiance in us. His red, drawn over the color of our blood-stained birth and our personal sins, changes our red into his radiance, by faith cleansing our hearts. Yes we have been justified by faith in the blood of Jesus.* Well does his blood poured out for you glow red for you, if it kindles in your spirit the desire to make some return. Well does his blood glow red for you, if the exceeding love of God gleams like red gold for you in the blood shed for you. Yes, Jesus so loved his bride that he washed her in his blood. Love is a red flame; it makes the Lord Jesus blood-red for me. In him truth is radiant for me and love is blood-red.

Rm 5:1, 9

'My Beloved,' says the bride, 'is radiant and blood-red.' Should he not be radiant? 'God is indeed the light and in him is no darkness.'* Should he not be blood-red? God is indeed the fire and came to cast fire upon earth.* If he offers you the light of understanding, for you he is radiant; but if he does not inflame your spirit to love, you do not experience him as blood-red. In himself he is both light and fire, but for you he is not light and fire except when you experience the effect of both. If you are a bride emulate the blending of this twofold color from your Bridegroom, that you may be alike radiant and blood-red, that is transparent and aflame. For as he possesses the power to clarify so also he has the power to set aflame. One who approaches him, approaches fire.*

1 Jo 1:5

Lk 12:49

Heb 1:29

'This is the end of Abbot Gilbert's *Sermones in Cantica*. Overtaken by death like Bernard, he could not complete them', Mab. He could not say: *Finis coronat opus*; that was left for John of Ford.[2] This incomplete sermon may have inspired 'The Burning Babe', a poem by the Elizabethan martyr, St Robert Southwell (1561–1595). Though allowed no writing materials in prison, Robert was allowed three favorite volumes, his breviary, a bible and his volume of St Bernard which he especially requested 'for his solace'; the volume may well have included Gilbert's 'sermons on the Canticle'.[3]

NOTES ON SERMON FORTY-EIGHT

1.   G. continues his instruction for one individual, though notice *videte* in par. 1. In the last sermons he shows no loss of vigor, no intention to discontinue. His abrupt ending is a surprise and suggests his realization that another would continue his work as he continued Bernard's work, the loving work of the Bridegroom.

2.   John of Ford, *Sermons on the Final Verses of the Song of Songs,* translated by Wendy Mary Beckett, Volume I (CF 29: Kalamazoo, 1977), others forthcoming. The critical edition by Edmund Mikkers and Hilary Costello appears in *Corpus Christianorum Continuatio Mediaevalis,* XVII & XVIII.

3.   See Pierre Janelle, *Robert Southwell the Writer* (London: Sheed and Ward, 1935) p. 68 and n. 35.

Gilbert of Hoyland

MIRA SIMPLICITAS

An unpublished earlier version of Sermons One and Two.

§

ABBREVIATIONS

The following abbreviations are used in the marginal notes of the edition:

B   the MS Bodley 24, used with permission of the Keeper of Western MSS, the Bodleian Library, Oxford.

BRa   where MSS Bodley 24 and Rawlinson G. 38 agree.

M   Migne, *Patres Latini*, vol. 184, edition of 1854.

Ra   the MS Rawlinson G. 38, used with permission of the Keeper of Western MSS, the Bodleian Library, Oxford. (Ra continues in the same hand with a work of Abbot Serlo of Savigny, on the Lord's prayer, beginning: *Servis Christi conservus eorum,* and ending: *dulcedo cordium, Jesus Christus, qui est Deus benedictus in saecula. Amen.*)

S   Gilbert's *Sermones* with number and paragraph in Migne.

Vulg.   reading of the Vulgate, *Biblia Sacra*, Rome: Desclée, 1927.

MIRA SIMPLICITAS

Cant 3:1

IN LECTULO MEO, PER NOCTES, QUAESIVI QUEM DILIGIT ANIMA MEA; QUAESIVI ILLUM ET NON INVENI*

1. Mira simplicitas sonat in verbis, piis suavitas auribus, et nescio, immo plane scio, quia mirabiliora sunt sacramenta quae latent. Reddunt me et mysteria stupidum et verba affectum et amatorio penitus afflatum blandimento. O quanta dulcedo in nucleo, si tanta redundat in cortice! Mysteria latent et cum labore eruuntur; verborum autem dulcedo in promptu est et ultro se offert, animis sine difficultate puris illapsa. Nos ergo non ita intendimus mysteriis, ut discedamus a modulis, cantica enim sunt et cantari malunt quam disputari, et nescio si evidentius possint edisseri quam cum cantantur. Favi enim sunt, et dum edisseruntur, cernuntur, dum cantantur, gustantur. Longe vero differenter respondet favi sapor palato, species oculo. Habent haec cantica laetis inmixta lugubria et gaudiis intextos gemitus, pro vario canentis affectu, sicut illa dilecto vel ex voto fruitur vel praeter votum fraudatur.*[1]

S 1:1, M 11A

2. Et nunc quod in manibus est, querulum quiddam sonare videtur et sponsi absentis causari

A WONDERFUL SIMPLICITY

IN MY LITTLE BED BY NIGHT I SOUGHT HIM
WHOM MY SOUL LOVES. I SOUGHT HIM AND
DID NOT FIND HIM.*   *Sg 3:1*

1. A wonderful simplicity rings out in these words,
charming to pious ears, and I know not whether, or
rather I know full well that the mysteries hidden
beneath the words are more wonderful.[1] I am
thunderstruck by the mysteries, full of affection at
the words, deeply inspired by the wooing of love.
O how much sweetness exists in the kernel, if so
much is tasted in the shell.[2] Mysteries lie hidden to
be dug out with effort, but the charm of the words
is on the surface, offered gratuitously, slipping without effort into pure souls. Now we do not so much
pay attention to the mysteries, as to disregard the
melody, for these are songs and prefer to be sung
rather than debated, and I know not whether they
can be analyzed more clearly than when they are
sung. Indeed they are honeycombs: when they are
analyzed they are seen by the eye, but when they
are sung they are savored by the tongue. In very
different ways does the taste of the honeycomb
tickle the palate and the sight of the honeycomb greet
the eye. These songs blend sorrow and joy, weave
grief with happiness, to correspond with the changing
affections of the singer, as now according to her wish
she enjoys her Beloved or again contrary to her wish
she is deprived of his presence.

2. Now in the verse we are discussing, the bride
seems to sing a plaintive song and to chide her Spouse

latebras, sic enim ait: 'in lectulo meo per noctes quaesivi quem diligit anima mea; quaesivi illum et non inveni'.* Dulce satis est te, bone Jesu, quaerere, dulcius tenere; in uno pius labor, plena in altero laetitia.* Si enim obvenit salus mulieri illi, felici furto tangenti fimbriam,* quid erit tenenti et amplexanti substantiam? Turba et premebat,* sed illa sola tangebat, forte quia turba se turbulenter ingessit, illa sobrie et silenter accessit. Illa te necdum a facie sed a posteriore tetigit,* et fluxus in ea sanguinis stetit. Stetit enim in ea omnis fluxus carnalis illecebrae, carnalis delectationis et curae, et restricta sunt et desiccata sunt, quae prius in ea fluxa et dissoluta et lascivientia erant, et totum hoc ad tactum fimbriae vestimenti tui. Plena benedictione huius* fimbria, descendit enim et defluxit unguentum de capite in oram vestimenti.* Ideo myrrha et gutta a vestimentis tuis;* myrrha quidem a vestimentis, sed myrrha prima a labiis, labia enim tua, lilia distillantia myrrham primam.* Quod si tanta in contactu fimbriae gratia, quid si caput ipsum amplexari contingeret, ex quo benedictionis tota effluxit ubertas? Non modo staret et exsiccaretur fluxus sanguinis sed statim emanaret impetus fluminis, illius utique qui laetificat civitatem Dei.*

3. *Felix, inquam, haec mulier et multum felix quae tetigit fimbriam, sed excellentius felix, quae amplius aliquid ausa gloriatur et dicit: 'fasciculus myrrhae dilectus meus mihi; in medio uberum meorum commorabitur'.* Talem sponsa frequenter experta complexum, elapsum rursus anxius quaerit. Audi quid loquitur: 'in lectulo meo per noctem quaesivi, quem diligit anima mea'.* Vide quomodo et locus et tempus negotio competit. 'In lectulo', inquit, 'meo quaesivi'; ibi enim potest investigari quietius, inveniri citius .et tutius teneri.* Quid ergo est aliud 'in lectulo' nisi in loco secreto et quieto? Jure illic,*

Marginal references (left column):

Sg 3:1

S 1:2; M 13A
Luc 8:44
B: premaebet;
Ra: premebat

BRa: posteriori

Ra: haec

Ps 132:2
Ps 44:9

Cant 5:13

Ps 45:4

Cant 1:12

Cant 3:1

S 1:2, M 13CD;
Ra: gap to par. 8.

for going into hiding, for these are her words: 'in my bed by night I sought him and did not find him'.* It is pleasant enough to seek you, good Jesus, more pleasant to hold you; to seek is the task of devotion, to hold is the fulness of joy. For if healing came to the woman who furtively touched the hem of your garment, what will take place in one who holds and embraces your substance! The crowd was pressing in upon you but she alone kept touching you, perhaps because the crowd rushed in riotously, while the woman approached soberly and silently. She touched you not yet from in front but from behind and the flow of blood was staunched. There stopped in her all the flow of carnal licentiousness, of carnal pleasure and anxiety; all that in her was once fluid and dissolute and wanton, was dammed and dried up, and all this at a touch of the hem of your garment. Full of blessings is the hem of his garment, for ointment falls and flows from his head to the hem of his garment.* Therefore myrrh and a drop [of aloes flows] from your garments,* myrrh indeed from your garments but prize myrrh from your lips, for your lips are lilies distilling prize myrrh.* If there was so much grace in the touch of the hem of his garment, what might have happened had she touched his very head from which has flowed the full bounty of his blessings! Not only would the flow have been staunched and the blood congealed, but straightway there would have been an overflow of that gushing stream which surely gladdens the city of God.*

3. Happy is this woman, I say very happy in touching the hem of his garment, but surpassing happy is the bride who boasts of having dared something more: 'a sachet of myrrh is my beloved to me that lies between my breasts'.* Having frequenlty experienced such an embrace, again she anxiously seeks him when he has slipped away. Hear what she says: 'Upon my little bed by night I sought him whom my soul loves'.* See how the time and the place are apt for their meeting. 'In my little bed', she says, 'I sought him', for there he can be traced more quietly, found more quickly and held more

Sg 3:1; S 1:2, M 13A.

Ps 132:2
Ps 44:9

Sg 5:13

Ps 45:5

Sg 1:12

Sg 3:1

Ps 75:3

Hebr 12:14

Jos 22:4

bone Jesu, quaereris, ubi libentius moraris. 'Factus est in pace locus' tuus, 'in pace locus' tuus 'et habitatio in Sion',* hoc est in pace et in speculatione. Praecedit pax, ut speculatio sequatur; 'pacem', inquit apostolus, 'sequamini', 'sine qua nemo videbit Deum'.* Jure ergo quietis delegit locum, quam amor ad quaerendum urgebat ardentior. Denique post curas cum quieti fuerimus redditi, acriorem sentimus morsum amoris divini.* Stupidum enim et insensibilem animum adversus huiusmodi stimulos mundi frequens cura solet efficere; idcirco dicit: 'in lectulo meo quaesivi quem diligit anima mea'. In loco certe brevi, immensum quaesivi, sed novit ipse breviorem se contrahere in modum et contemperare capacitati nostrae.

4. _'Quaesivi illum in lectulo meo'; mallem in suo, in illo amplo et intimo et occulto recessu et sinu Patris. Beatius plane ipsum penes seipsum cernerem, quem apud me quaererem; ibi enim in veritate et luce, hic in umbra et imagine, et ideo in nocte. 'Per noctem'. inquit, 'quaesivi.' 'In lectulo et per noctem quaesivi', ut habeam aliquem tactum dulcedinis etsi nondum luminis serenum. Potest enim hic dilectus magis suaviter sentiri, quam ad liquidum sciri; 'videmus nunc per speculum et in aenigmate', et quasi 'in_

1 Cor 13:12

nocte'.* Quod si per noctem est quod videmus, quanto magis quod quaerimus! Jure quidem, ubi lux quaeritur, nox commemoratur; neque enim posset lucem tenere et noctem tolerare. Bona tamen nox, quia tempus quietis, tempus absconsionis, tempus amoris aptum negotio. 'Abscondes eos in abscondito faciei tuae, a perturbatione hominum.'* 'Turbatus est', inquit, in via 'oculus meus.'* Bona huius ergo absconsio, quae dum a perturbatione protegit, purgat oculum, fovet aspectum et mentis aciem ad lucem praeparat.

Ps 30:21

Ps 6:6; Vulg.
a furore

securely.* What then is the meaning of 'in my little   S 1:2, M 13CD
bed', but in a hidden and quiet place? Rightly are
you sought there, good Jesus, where you dally more
deliberately. 'His abode has been established in peace
and his dwelling in Sion',* that is in peace and in con-   Ps 75:3
templation. Peace precedes, that contemplation may
follow; 'strive for peace', says the apostle, 'without
which no one will see God'.* Rightly then has she   Heb 12:14
chosen an abode of quiet, for a more ardent love was
urging her to seek. After anxieties, when we have
been restored to quiet as Scripture says,* we feel a   Jos 22:4
sharper sting of divine love. Frequent cares of the
world are wont to make the spirit dull and insensitive
to such goads; therefore the bride says: 'in my little
bed I sought him whom my soul loves'. Surely in a
limited abode I sought the unlimited, but he knows
how to limit himself to a smaller measure and to ad-
just to our capacity.

4. 'I sought him in my little bed', though my
preference is for his, in that spacious, intimate and
hidden retreat in the bosom of the Father. Yes I
would have a more blessed vision of him in his
home, whom I am seeking in mine, for there I would
see in truth and in light but here in shadow and in a
likeness, and therefore in night. 'By night I sought
him', says the bride. 'In my little bed and by night
I sought him', that I might have some touch of sweetness though not yet the brilliance of light. Here
indeed the Beloved can be experienced sweetly rather
than known transparently; 'now we see in a mirror
dimly', and as it were by night.* But if what we see is   1 Co 13:12
in the night, how much more what we seek! Rightly
then is the night mentioned when the light is being
sought, for one cannot both hold the light and endure
the night. Yet the night is good both as a time of
quiet and a time of hiding, a time suited to the exchange of love. 'In the covert of your presence you
will hide them from the disquiet of men.'* Again   Ps 30:21
the psalmist says: 'my eye was troubled' on the
way.* Good is the concealment of the bride, for   Ps 6:8
while protecting her from disquiet, it purifies her

5. *Melior talis nox die, sed illo de quo propheta:* 'diem hominis non concupivi, tu scis'.* Nescio quo pacto sibi adversantur et alterutro se·obscurant dies Domini et dies hominis, si quidem dum alter exoritur, alter reconditur.* 'Diem', inquit, 'hominis non concupivi', hoc est, humanum favorem, hominum gloriam, et inter reliquos, immo prae reliquis spectabilis videri.* Recte hunc diem propheta abjurat, qui perturbationis ministrat materiam.* Melior ergo haec nox die, si quidem nox a perturbatione abscondit, dies exponit. Denique primi parentes nostri, statim ut eorum oculi in hanc aperti sunt lucem, erubescentes confundebantur.* Nos quidem vereor, ne simila et forte ampliora passi, tali modo apertis oculis, caecatis animis, similiter* confundamur, non similiter erubescamus.* Quanto felicius clausa prius tenuere lumina et meliore cooperta nocte,* peccati nescientes pruriginem. Abinde sumpsit hic malus dies originem, qui vitiorum denudavit semitas, illicientes demonstravit species, concupiscentiae oculo sollicitantem ingessit materiam.*

6. *Heu me! quomodo me circumfulget dies ista!* quomodo affectum ad se meum abripuit; quomodo claro versantur in lumine ante mentis, oculos et quidem satis importune, impacata simul et impudica! Nusquam fere declinandi, nusquam delitescendi copia, nullae satis tutae sunt latebrae, ita ubique erumpunt et emergunt in cogitatum cuncta quae spiritum vel turbent vel turpent, sive diligenter attrectata, sive leviter tacta. Licet enim animus castigatiore repellat illa proposito, solo tamen sordidatur attactu, quo vel illa tangit vel tangitur ab illis. 'Qui tetigit picem, inquinabitur ab illa.'* Denique secundum legis scita, quarundam rerum tenuis etiam inquinat attactus, licet non ad culpam, ad aliquam tamen affectatae iniuriam munditiae.* Quid cum se contemplanti animo corporeae offunduntur imagines, non quae carnalem appetitum provocent, sed quae spiritualem

Margin notes:

Jer 17:16; Vulg. *desideravi*

S 1:4, M 14CD

3 Reg 17:17
B: *que*

Gen 3:7

B: *simi liciter*
B: *simi liciter*
B: *meliori*

S 1:4, M 15A.

Eccli 13:1

Lev 4:8

sight, and prepares the eye of her mind for the light.

5. Such a night is better than the day, but that day of which the prophet speaks: 'the day of man I have not desired, as you know'.* Somehow the day of the Lord and the day of man are opposed to each other, for when one dawns the other fades away. 'I have not desired the day of man', says the prophet, that is the applause of men, human glory, to be respected among others, even above others. Rightly the prophet renounces this day, because it provides a source of disquiet. This night is better than day, since night conceals a man from the disquiet to which the day exposes him. In Genesis, as soon as our first parents opened their eyes to this daylight, they blushed in confusion.* Yet I fear lest after similar or perhaps wider experiences, with eyes equally open but with closed minds, we may match them in confusion but match them in blushing for shame. How much happier were they pre-previously when they kept their eyes closed and when under cover of a better night they knew not sin's concupiscence. Thence this evil day drew its origin, for it laid bare the paths of vice, exposed alluring shapes and presented fascinating objects to the eye of concupiscence.*

Jr 17:16; S 1:4, M 14CD

Gn 3:7

S 1:4, M 15A.

6. Alas, how this day glitters around me, how it ensnared my affections! In what a naked light and how importunately do wild and wanton images together parade before the eyes of the mind! There is practically nowhere to turn aside, nowhere to hide; no hiding place is secure enough. From all sides there break and emerge into consciousness, whether deliberately welcomed or lightly brushed aside, all the images which trouble and defile the spirit. Though with stricter resolution the spirit may repel these images, still the spirit is sullied by the mere contact by which it either touches or is touched by them. 'Whoever touches pitch, will be defiled by it.'* According to the statutes of the Law, even the slightest contact with some objects causes defilement,* although not to our guilt, still with some harm to the purity we profess. What results when

Si 13:1

Lv 4:8

S 1:4, M 15A

contuitum tardent?* Nonne melius huiusmodi omnia obscurari quam illustrari? caeca obvolvi caligine quam clara et memori depromi in luce? Bona ergo nox,

B: *avertitur*

quae prudenti oblivione dissimulat et avertit* cuncta temporalia ad illum qui aeternus est quarendum tempus expediens et explicans occasiones, quae mundi

S 1:5, M 15BC

concupiscentiam abscondit, curam, cogitatum.* Hoc est enim mundum habere absconditum, vel mundo abscondi. Sic etiam abscondi poterimus in abscondito

Ps 30:21

faciei tuae, Domine,* non dico plena notione, sed tamen tota devotione et libera investigatione et aliquanta inventione. Hanc absconsionem, hoc secretum, has latebras quibus mundani diei declinamus vel amorem vel imaginationem, quibus humanum diem aut ablatum non repetimus aut oblatum respuimus, noctis nomine appelari nunc a sponsa crediderim.

7. *Denique in superioribus dicit: 'sub umbra eius quem desideraveram sedi, et fructus eius dulcis*

Cant 2:3

gutturi meo'.* Fructus iste suaviter pascit, si tamen prius umbra protraxerit. Bona umbra, quae carnis prudentiam obscurat et concupiscentiam refigerat. Intelligis quae sit umbra? Inde tibi refulget occasio quomodo et hic noctem intelligas, nisi quod quaedam occultiores latebrae et magis abditae, et accomodatae magis ad investigationis et contemplationis usum, sub noctis exprimuntur quam sub umbrae vocabulo. In umbra, rerum visibilium oblivionem aliquantam ac-

S 1:5, M 15D

cipe, in nocte omnimodam.* Hac ergo ratione, sponsa per noctem se quaerere dicit, quae reliqua iniusta nec respicit nec nota reputat, dum illum quem diligit intenta suspirat. Sed nos, fratres, quid in lectulo, quid per noctem, id est, quid in nostro vel occulto vel otio quaerimus? Utinam nihil* earum

B: *nichil*

quae pudore magis quam praedicatione digna sint, et operiri quam aperiri malint. Qui enim male agit,

Joan 3:20

odit lucem,* et quae in occulto aguntur, turpe est

images of the body pour into a contemplative spirit? Perhaps they do not arouse carnal desires but they do impede spiritual vision. Would not everything of the kind be better concealed than illustrated, better shrouded in an unseeing fog of oblivion than brought into the clear light of remembrance? Good then is the night, which in discreet forgetfulness disguises and turns aside all things temporal, scheduling a time and providing opportunities to seek that day which is eternal!* Good is the night, which hides the concupiscence, the care and the thought of the world. This is indeed to keep the world hidden or to be hidden from the world. We also can be so concealed 'in the covert of your presence',* O Lord, I do not say with full knowledge but with all devotion and free enquiry and some discovery. Our withdrawal, our concealment, our hiding places, whereby we shun either the love or the fancy of worldly daylight, whereby we do not retrieve the world's day once abandoned and scorn the world's day when proffered, these in my opinion are here termed night by the bride. *S 1:5, M 15BC*

Ps 30:21

7. In an earlier verse the bride says: 'I sat beneath the shadow of him whom I desired and his fruit was sweet to my palate'.* His fruit gives tasty nourishment, provided his shadow has previously given cover. Good is the shadow which conceals the prudence of the flesh and chills concupiscence. Do you understand the meaning of shadow? The passage on the shadow offers you a brilliant opportunity to understand our passage about night, except that some hiding places, better screened and camouflaged, more suited to the exercise of enquiry and contemplation, are expressed by the word 'night' rather than by 'shadow'. By the word 'shadow' understand some forgetfulness of the visible world and by the word 'night' total oblivion.* For this reason the bride says she seeks him by night, because she neither regards nor acknowledges the rest of the world, while she earnestly sighs for the one she loves. But what do we seek, my brothers, in our little bed and by night, that is, in our hiding place and our leisure? Hopefully, *Sg 2:3*

S 1:5, M 15D.

Eph 5:12   *et dicere.* *Haec vero quaesivit speciosum forma prae*
                filiis hominum; ideo gloriatur et dicit: 'in lectulo meo
Cant 3:1   *per noctes quaesivi, quem diligit anima mea'.**

8. *Putas autem quod mysterio vacet hoc ipsum*
S 2:1, M 17D   *quod dicit: 'in lectulo' et non 'in lecto'?* Ego quidem*
                crediderim quia noluit illud sibi exprobrari, quod per
                prophetam a Domino dicitur: 'dilatasti stratum tuum
Is 57:8; here   *iuxta me; suscepisti adulterum'.* Nos ergo non*
Ra: resumes   *dilatemus sed magis contrahamus stratum conscien-*
                tiae, cordis lectulum, et illud propheticum merito
                nobis coaptabitur: 'coangustatum est stratum ut
                alter decidat, et pallium breve utrumque operire non
Is 28:20   *potest'.* Breve enim et angustum est cor hominis ad*
                concipiendas vitales divini verbi delicias, etiam cum
S 2:1, M 18A   *in illas totum extenditur, nedum ad alia distentum.**
Ra: *illas in totum*   *Et ut ad simile vos provocem exemplum,*
BRa: *nichil*   *nihil* a vobis, fratres, vel studiose quaeratur vel*
                desidiosis ingeratur, quod sponsi offendat praesen-
                tiam, confundat conscientiam, conscientiam dico
1 Cor 10:29   *vestram, neque alterius.**

9. *Illud quoque observandum, quod dicit 'in*
                lectulo meo'. Alibi enim legis communiter dictum:
Cant 1:15   *'lectulus noster floridus'.* Forsitan est aliquis qui*
S 2:4-5, M   *solius sponsi sit lectulus.* Quis vero iste erit, nisi*
19B-20C   *alta illa et intima quies divinae bonitatis et sapientiae,*
Ra: omits   *illud aeternum tranquillitatis secretum et sacratum*
sacratum   *silentium, totiusque*. Trinitatis unitas et pax, 'quae*
Phil 4:7   *exsuperat omnem sensum!'* Et quidem 'multae*
Joan 14:2   *mansiones in domo Patris mei sunt';* Ipse vero*
1 Tim 6:16   *lucem habitat inaccessibilem;* denique summus ponti-*
Lev 16:17,   *fex sancta sanctorum solus ingreditur.* Et 'Patrem*
Heb 9:7   *nemo novit nisi Filius et cui ipse voluerit revelare'.**
*Matth 11:27   *Quod ergo paternum† novit Filius sicut ipse novit,*
†B: *patrem?*   *solius ipsius est et ceteris incommunicabile. Quan-*
Ra: *patrem.*

nothing which deserves shame rather than acclaim, which prefers to be concealed rather than revealed. For one 'who does evil, hates the light',* and deeds done in the dark 'it is shameful even to mention'.* But the bride sought the 'fairest in form among the sons of men'.* Therefore she boasts and says: 'in my little bed by night I sought him whom my soul loves'.*

Jo 3:20

Ep 5:12

Ps 44:3

Sg 3:1

8. Do you think her use of the diminutive is without hidden meaning, when she says 'in a little bed' and not 'in a bed'?* Personally I would suppose that she was unwilling to bear the reproach spoken by the Lord through the prophet: 'you have spread wide your couch beside me; you have welcomed an adulterer'.* Therefore let us not widen but rather narrow the couch of our conscience, the little bed of our heart. Then the verse of the prophet will be rightly applied to us: 'the couch is so narrow that the one or the other may fall out, and the short blanket cannot cover both'.* Indeed the heart of man is confined and narrow in welcoming the living delights of God's word, even when man's heart is wide open for those delights and far from being open to other delights. To challenge you to emulate her example, let nothing be earnestly sought by you, brothers, or undertaken among the idle, which might offend the presence of the Bridegroom or confound one's conscience, 'I mean your own, not the conscience of another'.*

S 2:1, M 17D

Is 57:8

Is 28:20; S 2:1, M 18A.

1 Co 10:29

9. The pronoun she uses should also be noticed, 'in my little bed'.* Elsewhere you read of a shared bed; 'our little bed is all flowers'.* Perhaps there is a little bed reserved for the Bridegroom alone. But what will this be, if not that deep and intimate quiet of the divine goodness and wisdom, that eternal, secret and sacred silence of tranquillity, the unity and peace of the whole Trinity 'which surpasses all understanding'.* Yes indeed, 'in my Father's home there are many rooms',* but he 'dwells in unapproachable light',* and the high priest enters the holy of holies alone.* 'And no one knows the Father except the Son and anyone to whom the Son wishes to reveal him.'* What the Son knows about the

*S 2:4-5, M 19B-20C. *Sg 1:15*

Ph 4:7

Jo 14:2

1 Tm 6:16

Lv 16:17, Heb 9:7

Mt 11:27

tum nobis revelare dignatur, in secreti nos sui cubiculum ex parte admittit, et quietis suae communicat lectulum.

10. *Illum vero quem suum sponsa lectulum vocat, vide si non recte rationalis animae possit accipi natura; huius enim divinae essentiae in se obtinet imaginem, sed non veritatem. Cum ergo ex propriae consideratione naturae divinam vel quaerit vel contemplatur substantiam, ut in umbra et imagine veritatem inveniat, tunc istud dicere non incongrue poterit, de quo nunc agitur: 'in lectulo meo per* noctes* *quaero quem diligit anima mea'. 'Quem diligit', inquit, non 'quem metuit', semper enim quem timemus horremus, quem amamus optamus, nec possumus eius optare praesentiam, cuius formidamus sententiam. Dilectio vero super meritum extendit votum; immo idem illi est, votum et meritum, 'finis enim praecepti caritas de corde puro et conscientia bona'.* Nescit caritas bona carere conscientia, si quidem caritas nihil perperam agit,* et quae perperam gesta sunt, operit.* Nil bona tutius conscientia: bona conscientia audet et caritas ardet; illa non formidat, ista inflammat; illa pro delicto non confundit, ista super dilecto confidit.* Magna vis amoris: alieno non nititur suffragio, propriis contenta meritis; semper amari se praesumit, quae amara se sentit; denique, non respectis aliis maiestatis nominibus, solum sponsa dilectum memorat,* quae singulariter intus tolerat aestus amoris. Hoc autem attendendum, quam* frequenter dilecti recenset vocabulum,† quocumque ex mysterio: 'dilectus meus candidus et rubicundus',* et 'talis est dilectus meus',* et in praesenti, 'quem diligit anima mea'.* Magna certe sermonis huius gratia, nec mirum si frequentatur in ore, quod fervet in corde. Ideo et animam commemorat, non enim verbo tantum diligit sed voto, nec solo actu sed magis affectu.**

Ra: *noctesque*

1 Tim 1:5
1 Cor 13:4
1 Petr 4:8

S 1:7, M 16CD

Ra: *nominat et memorat*
*Ra: *quod*
†S 1:8, M 17A
Cant 5:10
Cant 5:16
Cant 3:1

S 1:7, M 17A

Father, then, exactly as the Son knows, belongs to the Son alone and is incommunicable to others. As far as the Son thinks fit to make a revelation to us, he admits us partially into the chamber of his hiding place and shares the little bed of his repose.

10. But consider whether the little bed which the bride calls her own, might not rightly be understood as the nature of the rational soul, for it contains in itself the image though not the reality of his divine essence. When therefore from a consideration of its own nature, the soul seeks or contemplates the divine substance, in order to discover the divine reality in its shadow and image, the soul will then be able to utter without inconsistency the verse we are discussing: 'in my little bed by night I seek him whom my soul loves'. 'Whom my soul loves', are her words, not 'whom my soul fears', for we always shun the one we fear but long for the one we love, nor can we long for the presence of one whose judgment we dread. Perfect love indeed extends its longing beyond its merit, or rather, for perfect love longing and merit are the same thing, for 'the aim of our charge is charity arising from a pure heart and a good conscience'.* Charity presupposes the presence of a good conscience, since charity does nothing falsely,* and charity covers what has been done falsely.* Nothing is more secure than a good conscience.* A good conscience is bold for its love is not cold; it lives without fright for love sets it alight; it does not blush for a fault for love trusts the Beloved. Great is the power of love. Love does not rely on another's favor but is satisfied with its own deserts. Conscious that it loves, it assumes that it is always loved. In the Canticle, disregarding his other titles of distinction, the bride mentions only her 'Beloved', because in a special way she endures within, the ardor of his love. Notice how frequently, whatever the mystery, she recalls the word 'Beloved';* 'my Beloved is radiant and ruddy',* and 'such is my Beloved',** and in the present verse, 'whom my soul loves'.* Great surely is the charm of this word. It is no surprise if what glows in her heart overflows from her lips. For this reason

1 Tm 1:5

1 Co 13:4

1 P 4:8

S 1:7, M 16CD

S 1:8, M 17A.
*Sg 5:10
**Sg 5:16
*Sg 3:1

11. *Quid vero sibi vult, quod 'animam', non
'spiritum' dicit? Forte quia dilecto quem adhuc
quaerebat, nondum adhaerebat, 'qui enim adhaeret*

Ra: *Deo et Domino* *Domino,* unus est spiritus'.** Et quidem nusquam*
**1 Cor 6:17 *in toto hoc cantico spiritum nominat, sed 'anima
mea liquefacta est',* et 'anima mea conturbavit*
Cant 5:6 *me',* et hoc ipsum frequenter: 'quem diligit anima*
Cant 6:11 *mea',* id quoque fere nusquam nisi cum absentem*
Cant 3:1 *quaerit, vel abesse queritur. Solent his nominibus
gradus quidam distingui animae perfectioris et minus
perfectae. Apostolus dicit: 'animalis homo non per-*
1 Cor 2:14 *cipit quae sunt spiritus Dei'.* Ego animam hanc ita
amantem et aestuantem, ferventem et quaerentem,
nunquam non spiritualem dixerim, quippe quae
licet nondum plena visione, voto tamen propenso*
S 1:8, M 17BC *illi adhaerebat, quem vehementer diligebat.**

12. *Possumus autem non incongrue, sicut in
spiritu, subtilem et attenuatum intellectum, sic in
anima, suavem et tenerum accipere affectum. Per
prophetam in promissione Dominus dicit: 'dabo*
Ez 11:19 *vobis cor carneum';* si ergo carnis nomen in bono
alicubi accipitur, cur non magis animae? Ego beatam
hanc animam, ut licenter loquar, non corneam sed
carneam magis iudicaverim, et nil habentem in se
rigoris vel duritae, sed mollem, teneram, tractabilem
et sensibilem ad singulos divini verbi aculeos, denique*
Job 6:12 *ut dicat: 'neque caro mea aenea est,'* sed quam*
Luc 2:35 *spiritualis pertranseat gladius,* et caritate se vulnera-*
Ps 44:6 *tam gaudeat. Sagittae eius acutae sunt,* et leniter
illabuntur animo, et sine laesione ad intima penetrant,
et statum mentis inebriant, et in quosdam inexpertos
et insperatos commutant affectus, nisi quod caritas*
1 Cor 13:7 *'omnia sperat',* et eorum quae iam percepit argu-
mento, maiora sibi pollicetur.*

also she refers to her soul, for she loves not only in word but also in her heart, not in deed alone but especially in affection.

11. Now what is meant by her mention of 'soul' rather than 'spirit'? Perhaps because she did not yet cling to her Beloved whom she was still seeking, for 'he who clings to the Lord is one spirit with him'.* *1 Co 6:17* Indeed nowhere in the entire Canticle does she mention the word 'spirit', but she says, 'my soul melted',* and 'my soul was troubled',** and frequently as in the present verse, 'he whom my soul loves'.* Even this verse she almost never uses except when she seeks him in his absence or complains of his absence. By these terms several degrees of perfection are usually distinguished: a soul more perfect and a soul less perfect. The apostle says: 'an unspiritual man does not receive the gifts of the Spirit of God'.* Personally I would never call unspiritual, this soul so ardently in love and so fervent in her quest, for although still without full vision yet with ever increasing desire she clings to him whom she passionately loves.

Sg 5:6
**Sg 6:11*

Sg 3:1

1 Co 2:14, S:18, M 17BC.

12. As we can aptly consider 'spirit' to mean a subtle and refined understanding, so we can consider 'soul' to mean a gentle and tender affection. The Lord promises us through the prophet: 'I will give you a heart of flesh'.* If then in some passage, the word 'flesh' is understood in a good sense, why not still more the word 'soul'? If I may speak freely, I would personally consider this blessed soul not one of horn but rather of flesh, having nothing stubborn or harsh but being soft, tender, pliable and sensitive to every dart from the divine Word, so that with Job it may say 'not of bronze is my flesh',* but flesh which the sword of the spirit may pierce,* and which may rejoice in having been wounded by charity. The arrows of the word are sharp,* and slip gently into the spirit, without mortal wound penetrate to its depths, change the mind to a state of inebriation and transform it with affections beyond experience and expectation, except that 'charity hopes for all things',* and on the strength of what charity already

Esk 11:19

Jb 6:12
Lk 2:35

Ps 44:6

1 Co 13:7

*13. Felix plane cor, in quo omnis emollita est
duritia et rigor et insensibilitas, spiritus calefacta et
animata alloquio, ignitum enim eloquium eius vehe-*

Ps 118:140
Ps 54:22

menter, et 'molliti sunt sermones eius super oleum,
et ipsi sunt jacula'.* 'Oleum', inquit, et 'jacula',
perungunt enim et compungunt, sauciant et sanant,
instigant et mitigant; mitigant tumorem, instigant ad
amorem. Oleum sunt, dum sensim et non sine mora
intrant in interiora; jacula vero, propter amoris
impetum et impatientiam desiderii anxie concupi-
scentis et aegre carentis. Oleum quia leniter et lente
mentem inficit; jaculum, quia transitorio sed in-
tolerabili amoris ictu sentientem consumit paene et
conficit. In oleo, dulcis et diuturnior sensus; in
jaculo, vehemens sed velox excessus. Propter huiusmodi animam dicit quia sit spiritualis amoris succensa
igniculo, saucia jaculo, fota oleo, informata eloquio.*

SUPER HESTERNO CAPITULO

*14. Super hesterno capitulo, hodernum vobis in-
stauramus convivium, nec enim ibi cuncta dicta sunt*

S 2:1, M 17C

quae dicenda occurrunt. Et primo non satis admirari
possum de ipsa clausularum serie et consequentiae*

S 1:1, M 11A

rerum. Quae enim ordinis ratio, ut sponsa tam dilecta,
tam docta, quaerat in lectulo quem salientem proxime
reliquit in montibus, quaerat in plateis quem pascen-*

Cant 2:16-17

tem proponit in liliis? Stupenda plane ratio, ut
inter angustias requirat lectuli, qui libertate montium,
caprearum levitate vaga perfruitur! Si figuris istis
spiritualium proponitur series et ordo profectuum,
valde quidem reconditus est, affectum vero varietas
manifesta. Ubi profectus docetur tenor quidam et
gradata servatur dispositio; ubi loquitur affectus et
amor, libera passim lege vagatur, et quod prius*

perceives, promises itself still greater gifts.

13. Obviously happy is the heart, in which has been softened all harshness and stubbornness and insensitivity, after being warmed and enlivened by the exhortation of the spirit whose eloquence burns with passion,* and whose 'words are softer than oil although they are arrows'.* His words are 'oil' and 'arrows' says the psalmist, for they are both unction and compunction, they cut and they cure, they are a spur and a bridle, a bridle for our pride and a spur for our love. They are oil when gently and without haste they seep into our interior, but they are arrows no less, thanks to the impetuosity of love and the impatience of longing, when the lover fondly frets and grows wan with waiting. Yes they are oil, because imperceptibly and slowly they penetrate the mind, but arrows because with the transient and intolerable wound of love they almost devour and destroy their victim. In oil there is a sweet and more lasting experience, in arrows a fiery but fleeting ecstasy.* Thanks to a soul of this kind, the bride says she is aflame with an ember of spiritual love, wounded by an arrow, soothed with oil and formed by eloquence.

Ps 118:140
Ps 54:22

G. avoids ecstasis

SUPER HESTERNO CAPITULO

14. From yesterday's passage let me celebrate with you the banquet of today.[3] First, I cannot sufficiently wonder at the very series of the clauses and the sequence of events. What is the explanation of this order, that the bride, so beloved and so experienced, should seek in her little bed for one whom she recently left leaping upon the mountains,* and that she should seek in the squares for one she envisions grazing among lilies?* Obviously amazing is the explanation of why she seeks within the confines of her little bed for one who enjoys the freedom of the mountains and the carefree nimbleness of gazelles. If in these figures a sequence and order of spiritual progress is envisioned, it is well hidden indeed, though the variety of the bride's affections is mani-

Sg 2:17

Sg 2:16

erumpit in animum, eructat in canticum. Non est autem nunc nostri vel otii vel ingenii, omnes carminis huius clausulas consequentem et evidentem summatim digerere in seriem. Propterea relicta hac communi summa, redeamus ad singula.

15. '*In lectulo meo per noctes quaesivi.' Bonus plane lectulus de quo legis in proberbiis: 'secura mens quasi juge convivium';* foris nox, foris turbatio, sed tranquillitas intus, quasi quietis lectulus quidam.* Non est hic illud lamentabile dicere: 'foris interficit gladius et domi mors similis est'.* Immo si foris gladius, intus gaudium: 'spe', inquit, 'gaudentes, in tribulatione patientes'.* Ad noctem tribulatio refertur, ad lectulum spes et gaudium. Forte propter hoc non lectum sed lectulum parco appellat vocabulo, quoniam totum gaudium nostrum fere in spe est adhuc et ex parte.*²*

Prov 15:15
S 2:2, M 18BC

Lam 1:20

Rom 12:12

S 2:2, M 18C

fest. When some sequence of events in perfect harmony is being explained, then step by step the order of events is maintained; but when affection and love is the singer, then the tune wanders here and there with a law of its own, and what first breaks in upon the spirit, bursts into song. Now however, it is beyond either my leisure or my talent, to arrange by way of summary all the clauses of this Canticle into an orderly and obvious sequence. Therefore abandoning a general summary, let us return to the individual clauses of the Canticle.

15. 'In my little bed by night I sought him.'* Good obviously is the little bed of which you read in Proverbs: 'a carefree mind is a perpetual feast';* outside is the night, outside the hurricane, but inside is tranquillity like a little bed of repose. Here there is no need to repeat the lament: 'outside the sword slays and indoors is like a death'.* Rather, if outside is the sword, inside is rejoicing, 'rejoicing in hope', says the apostle, 'patient under tribulation'.* Tribulation is attributed to the night, hope and rejoicing to the little bed. Perhaps for this reason the bride says not 'a bed', but 'a little bed', the diminutive term, because practically all our rejoicing is still in hope and imperfect.[4]

Sg 3:1, S 2:2, M 18BC.

Pr 15:15

Lm 1:20

Rm 12:12

NOTES ON *MIRA SIMPLICITAS*

1. Bodleian Ms 24, of the 12th-13th century, contains G.'s Epistles, *Epistolae Gilleberti Quondam Abbatis Hoylandiae,* his *Tractatus,* and his incomplete *Sermo* on the sower, and immediately following in the same first hand, ff. 96v-106v, beginning *Mira simplicitas,* is what Jean Leclercq considered perhaps a first draft of the *Sermones* as finally printed; see 'La première rédaction des *Sermones in Cantica* de Gilbert de Hoyland', RB 62 (1952) 289-90, and Mikkers 272. In the first *Sermones* as finally printed, G. changed the emphasis from *simplicitas* to *affectus amantium,* but he returned frequently to *simplicitas* later: S16:5, 22:3, 5, 41:1, 43:3. Here, apparently in a first printing in any language of *Mira simplicitas,* references are given to the *Sermones* where many sentences are identical, and an enumeration of paragraphs has been added for convenient reference.

2. De Lubac I:603, nn. 2-3, lists early authors who mention the nut and the honeycomb to distinguish the literal and the spiritual senses of scripture; some of these authors may have been familiar to Gilbert, Origen for example in the translation of Rufinus. G. does not mention the nut elsewhere nor the honeycomb in this meaning, though he returns to the honeycomb elsewhere at length: Ep 2:2-3, T 4:3-5, S 41:3-7, where he comments on Sg 4:11 and 5:1. He is obviously thinking of Pr 16:24, 'favus mellis composita verba', and Pr 24:13, where wisdom is 'favum dulcissimum gutturi tuo' and perhaps Lk 24:42. See my article, 'The Honeycomb in Gilbert of Hoyland' in CSt 14 (1979).

3. S 2:1, M 17C. The first letter is capitalized as if to begin a second sermon.

4. The text of *Mira simplicitas* ends here.